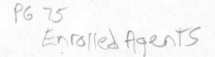

DIVORCE AND MONEY

Everything You Need to Know

DIVORCE
and MONEY

Everything You Need to Know

GAYLE ROSENWALD SMITH, J.D.

A PERIGEE BOOK

P

A Perigee Book
Published by The Berkley Publishing Group
A division of Penguin Group (USA) Inc.
375 Hudson Street
New York, New York 10014

Copyright © 2004 by Gayle Rosenwald Smith, J.D.
Cover design by Liz Sheehan
Text design by Kristin del Rosario

First edition: January 2004

ISBN: 0-399-52943-8

Visit our website at
www.penguin.com

This book has been cataloged by the Library of Congress

Printed in the United States of America
10 9 8 7 6 5 4 3 2 1

To my father, Judge Edward Rosenwald (1910–1998)
and my mother, Ruth Rosenwald (1921–1999),
whose passion and respect for one another continue to inspire me.

To David, my soul mate,
who shares my passions and my life.

To Rachel and Aaron,
who daily expand the meaning of love. YMLWL.

To Sheila Curry Oakes,
who has been there every step of the way.

ACKNOWLEDGMENTS

I would like to thank the following attorneys who helped me in this endeavor. Susan V. Edwards of Pennsylvania, family lawyer and mediator extraordinaire, who, despite an overwhelmingly busy schedule, read the manuscript and gave willingly of her time and ideas. Alan Koritzinsky of Wisconsin tirelessly steered me toward key people I interviewed and graciously provided me with information on a wide variety of topics. Norma Levine Trusch continued to be an invaluable resource for this book as well as for the last one. Joy Fineberg of Illinois, Richard Podell of Wisconsin, and Ronald Nelson of Kansas helped with differences in the state laws. One collective thank-you goes to all the other attorneys, too numerous to mention, who gave graciously of their time to help ensure the accuracy of the law in different states.

Thanks, too, go to Jeremy G. Gabell, CPA, for his invaluable advice on the financial end. Nancy Dimmick offered her financial acumen. Stacey Collins gave generously of her time and knowledge of business valuations. Stuart Kahn helped with insurance issues.

I wish to thank the many family law judges throughout the country who spoke with me and offered their advice and opinions on money and divorce. They enlightened me about regional differences and regional trends.

Dr. Judith Shechter helped immensely with the emotional challenges presented by divorce.

Thanks to my friends and readers—Anne Weiss, Christine Dietrich, and Richard Fishel, who gave me valuable insights. Overwhelming thanks to John Timpane for all his help and advice.

A special thanks goes to my family and friends, who are always there for me. And to Allan Wolfe—you mean the world to me.

CONTENTS

INTRODUCTION

Being a divorce attorney has given me a healthy respect for the divorce process. No one escapes its ill effects—the rich, the famous, and the least wealthy are equally devastated. It is not a process to step into lightly, without thought, introspection, and planning. Unlike most events in your life, experiencing a divorce will make you re-think your values and beliefs.

As a family lawyer, a concern of primary importance is to avoid the breakup of a marriage if at all possible. The very first question I ask any client is, "Are you sure your marriage is over?" If, after asking this question of yourself as well as much probing and soul-searching, you can honestly say you are sure the marriage is not worth saving, then you need to get mentally prepared and financially ready to undertake the most important business deal of your life. If children are involved, concern for their well-being may overshadow financial issues. But children or not, you also must face an important issue that could have a profound impact on the rest of your life—securing your financial future and establishing your economic health.

A VIEW FROM THE BENCH

A very wise judge from the Southwest told me, "Marriage is all about love. Divorce is all about money! The hardest thing about trying to divide property when a marriage ends is that we are all fools in love. It has nothing to do with class or education. Logic just doesn't rule. And that's the very thing that should rule."

For many years now, men and women have been coming to me for advice about how to get out of their marriages without going broke. That's the goal of a "good" divorce. Some clients have been financially savvy; others haven't known how to write a check. One and all were overwhelmed. No one knows where to begin to get their financial household in order. After years of listening to clients, I have learned the value of educating them about their financial rights and responsibilities. It is important to know just what information is essential, how to go about obtaining it, and what to do with it.

This book will take you step by step through the issues you need to master so your divorce settlement will bring you the most cash, assets, and financial support to make the transition into a new life a lot easier.

BEING PRACTICAL

Getting started means gaining an understanding of what typically happens in a divorce. Most property division starts with a fifty-fifty split—one spouse receiving 50 percent of the assets and the other spouse receiving the other 50 percent. This rule may not be written in rule books, but most fact-finders admit that's the starting point. (A fact-finder is any one of a number of people including hearing officers, masters, and judges who will listen to your case and decide the outcome of the different issues. In many states, hearing officers who may or may not be attorneys, may hear your case and make an initial decision. A master who is generally a lawyer may review the hearing officer's decision or may make an initial decision before the case reaches a judge. You may want to check with a lawyer to find out the procedure in your state.) From that point fact-finders move on to ask, "Is there any compelling reason to deviate from this percentage?" You need to focus on the answer to that question, which in turn brings up others: 50 percent of what? What's fair? Who needs what? Who deserves what?

The problem with divorce is that after living so long with a person you loved, you have learned which buttons to push. When you divorce, it is tempting to use this knowledge and take out your anger and forget about being rational. When it comes to money and divorce, however, that impulse spells disaster. Divorce means division of property. Revenge should take a backseat. This has to be a cool, rational business deal.

This book will help you navigate through this treacherous emotional terrain so you can focus on your task at hand. Whatever psychological meaning money may have for you, the only thing it should represent to you in your business deal is how much you will have to start your new life.

A good divorce takes planning. This book will guide you

through the planning stage and into the action stage. In a divorce, you need to understand how to partner—ideally with a lawyer and other advisers—to determine what property you and your spouse acquired during your marriage. Most clients get hung up on the question, "What things do I want?" The emotionally driven answer to that question is typically, "My spouse will only get those things over my dead body!" It is essential to look at the big picture. If you can't logically and rationally identify all the "things" you own, you will lose the opportunity to fight for them.

You need to be proactive and plan your moves. As much as you might like to be rid of your spouse right now, you can't leave without an exit strategy or a series of steps you will need to take before you think of getting out of the marriage. This book helps you set up such a strategy.

You need to list all your property—not only the property you both acquired during marriage, but also the property you and your spouse brought to the marriage. Often, getting a complete list requires sleuthing. It would be ideal if you inventoried all your property before you were married and during the marriage. However, few couples do so.

You need a basic understanding of the "things" to which you are entitled. Do you and your spouse work? Are you aware of how much each is paid for that work? What does payment include? Salary? Pension? Stock options? Other perks? How is this compensation valued?

THE ART OF THE DEAL

In many respects, ending a marriage is no different from splitting a business. You need to ask yourself, "How can I get out of this marriage and remain financially secure?" Start by learning the ins and outs of your finances. My job is made significantly easier (and my client's bill a lot less expensive) when my clients do their homework while they are still in the relationship. It's also a lot easier to do this homework while you are still living under the same roof.

In preparing this book, I spent a great deal of time interviewing judges and lawyers nationwide and have presented their suggestions on how to approach divorce matters. Laws and the application of the rules vary from state to state, so be certain you check with a lawyer in your state to learn the law and how it applies to the facts of your case.

You will need to be armed with knowledge of many concepts. For example, you need to know the meaning of marital estate: what you will be splitting. You will need to understand, from the most elementary concepts to the most sophisticated, what property may be involved in your divorce.

MASTERING THE PAPERWORK

You have a lot of paperwork to complete. You need to know how much money comes into your house each month, where the money is coming from and where it is going, who is bringing the money in, and what other income or monies might qualify as property that needs to be split. You might believe your spouse is taking money and hiding it somewhere so you won't be able to get it if you divorce. To discover any hidden funds or assets, you need to be able to reconstruct the numbers that support your lifestyle.

FINDING A LAWYER

Lawyers can make a difference. If you don't have enough money to use a lawyer throughout the entirety of your case, you should, at least, gather all the pertinent information and consult with a lawyer. Figuring out the marital estate and then getting 50 percent of that, let alone more, may take creative lawyering. A good lawyer can help you identify the issues in your case. How do you find a good lawyer? How do you keep from spending so much on legal fees that nothing is left to divide? Finding the right lawyer may take time, but it is worth the investment.

A good, honest lawyer can work with you as your partner to help you define how your property should be split, define the issues and identify the issues that can help you get your fair share, and help point you in the right direction to get good financial advice.

FINDING THE RIGHT EXPERTS

At some point, you may want to consider hiring experts to help you come to a decision on a good property split. Your experts may include a financial consultant or a good accountant to help you review essential financial documents. If you or your spouse own a business, you may need a business valuator to help determine how much the business is worth. You may also need help to find out if your spouse is using the business to hide money. Or maybe you need a tax consultant to give advice on whether it is more advantageous to choose one piece of property in the marital estate rather than another.

THE QUESTION OF THE HOUSE

In many marriages, the marital home is often one of the largest assets and the one that sparks the most angst. Clients always ask, "Should I stay or should I leave the house?" The answer to that question depends on the situation. Are you in any physical danger if you stay? Do you have all of the necessary financial information? Is your spouse about to receive a large bonus you stand to lose your fair share of if you leave? Your emotions may be telling you that under no circumstances will you sell the house that pro-

vides you and your children the stability you crave at the moment. But your finances may give you a different message.

KNOWING YOUR WORTH

To get a fair deal, you need to know what your assets are worth. Whether you need to know the value of your house or the value of a business, you need to understand the fundamentals of property valuation. Think of your divorce as a business course. You need to educate yourself. The only way you can fight properly for your future economic security is to have the power that comes from knowledge and the tools to implement that knowledge.

Does your spouse work for a company and get a pension or stock options? You need to know what part of those benefits rightfully belong to you. You also need to know how much the benefits are worth. Different methods of valuation can be used to determine their worth.

You may have to get an expert to determine the value of certain property. It is important for you to understand what the expert will be doing. At the very least, you need to be familiar with the terms and what they mean. Ultimately, your understanding of these terms will translate into dollars and cents.

UNDERSTANDING RETIREMENT PLANS

Retirement may be the last thing on your mind right now. Worrying about balancing the checkbook today may be overwhelming enough. When your marriage was working, perhaps you assumed you could rely on your spouse to help support you in retirement. Too often one spouse has socked away cash for retirement while the other spouse has faithfully paid the everyday expenses and put off saving. You will need to learn about retirement plans and what the differences among them may mean to you. How can you get your fair share?

ALIMONY AND CHILD SUPPORT

If you have given up work to raise children or to help advance your spouse's career, are you entitled to spousal support or alimony?

If you have children, you will want to know how much child support you might expect to receive or pay. What does child support include? Who pays for a child's medical insurance? What about dental and counseling bills? There are certain minimum state guidelines the courts use to determine the amount of child support owed. Again, every case is different, and you'll need to know what extras to identify and whether you can expect to get or pay more or less than the minimum.

HOW DIVORCE AFFECTS YOUR FUTURE

Divorce can have an unexpected but very real effect on your life. For example, suppose you are unhappy in your job and want to make a change. Once you have a family to support and decide to divorce, you may not have the luxury of making the decision to change jobs or careers. You may be compelled to maintain a certain level of income once support becomes an issue. Courts may step in and make certain decisions in your life when you are divorcing. Suppose you hate your job and you want to quit and take a lesser-paying one. You may have to pay child support based on the higher level of income. You may not even be aware of all the possible contingencies and how they could affect your future. Know the steps that you need to take to protect yourself.

Divorcing couples are often faced with no assets and a great deal of debt. Under these circumstances, you will have decisions to make. You may want to seek the advice of a consumer credit counselor or a bankruptcy lawyer. Again, you will need to do your homework and make certain that you have a comprehensive list of all outstanding debts. How can you best protect yourself from a creditor looking to you to pay a debt that your spouse incurred during marriage?

TO COURT OR NOT TO COURT?

Fighting in court is not always the answer. You need to weigh carefully just who it is that you want to make the major decisions about your future. My father was a lawyer and then became a judge. Growing up, I was always fascinated with listening to lawyers and judges talk about their profession. I learned that judges are human beings with biases and prejudices and strong opinions. As a lawyer, I also learned that once cases are fully and properly prepared, you should consider all the alternative dispute-resolution options.

Legal fees can get quite expensive. You need to make an educated decision: Should you go for the jugular, or should you decide what you need to live, what you think you could get in court, and what you are willing to take in settlement? All options should be weighed. You can decide only after having fully reviewed all the documentation necessary. In addition, you should add in the emotional cost of going to court.

IT'S WORTH IT

All this preparation and education may seem like a daunting task. However, if you take it one step at a time and do the necessary fact-finding, you'll start learning what you need to start a new life with a more secure economic future. It may not seem possible now, but when you look back, you will be amazed at how much you have learned and how much more in control of your life you are.

This book is organized in sections. You will probably want to read it through and then reread relevant sections again and again.

Here's a "to-do" list as you approach the difficult process of divorce:

1. *Figure out whether divorce is the correct option. Answer the difficult question: "Is my marriage worth saving?"*

2. *Focus on money. Divorce is a business deal.*

   ▪ *What property do we own?*

   ▪ *To whom do we owe money?*

3. *Determine how much the marital estate is worth. What is the value of all the property?*

4. *Master the paperwork.*

   ▪ *How do I go about finding out what property we own?*

   ▪ *How much money comes into the house each month, and how much money goes out and to whom?*

5. *Decide what expert advice you need. Find out how to locate the best expert advisers.*

6. *Decide which route is best to resolve the divorce issues.*

I hope you find this book an indispensable companion as you navigate through the turbulent waters of your divorce. Consider this guidebook a compass to help you chart your way through this difficult time.

Chapter One

THE BUSINESS DEAL: THERE'S NO ROOM FOR EMOTION

Ending the financial part of your marriage is no different from ending a business relationship. If you walk away from this book with a mantra, it should be the following:

Focus on the Money

You need to separate your emotional state from your financial state. Splitting property is a matter of dollars and cents. A good financial settlement in a divorce is based solely on the numbers.

Judges nationwide endorse the principle that you need to keep your emotions in check while going through the divorce process—especially the business end.

A VIEW FROM THE BENCH

A judge from the mid-Atlantic region says, "Among all the situations involving anguish, heartbreak, and anger, I have seen the most among spouses, partners, and, surprisingly, friends. I have said to more people than I can count, 'Take a few minutes to collect yourself, because if during this period, you can keep your attention on the things that really count, you will have a better success rate in the litigation. Remember to focus, focus, focus.'"

The judge also recommends that you make an honest emotional assessment of your relationship with your spouse. If you are certain there is no possibility of reconciliation, move on with your life sooner rather than later. This approach during the legal process will help you improve your focus. Finally, keep this pain separate from the business end of the case. As the judge says, "Stay calm, study the whole situation, and work toward a realistic financial goal."

If you are angry (and a lot of people are), get it over with before you make your business deal. Redirect your anger into constructive bargaining.

Anyone who has gone through a divorce truly appreciates that divorce is a process that takes place over time. It doesn't begin with the filing of a complaint and end with a divorce decree. It begins when you are unhappy. The unhappiness grows until finally you know you can't spend the rest of your life with your present partner. Or perhaps, it may begin more abruptly, with your partner telling you that he or she is unhappy, or has a new love, and the marriage is over. Either way, the divorce process generally takes longer than either of you would like it to last. (One couple who were married for only two weeks took four years to dissolve the union. They were so emotionally involved in the process that they weren't able to let go of the marriage.)

A psychological process parallels the legal. Going through a divorce is similar to living life on a constant roller-coaster ride. One minute you're up, and the next you're plunged into deep despair. Along with unhappiness comes denial. You may then get angry— angry about the financial burdens your spouse is loading you with, furious at your spouse for screwing up your life and those of your children (if you have a family), or angry at him or her for causing your present life—however wretched it may be—to end.

These feelings are all very common when a marriage is breaking up. From a financial perspective, however, you can never negotiate your business deal until you are ready to take emotion out of the bargaining.

If your spouse is the one who announces the marriage is over, you may find yourself instantly behind psychologically and legally. Usually, the spouse who decides the marriage is over will have gone through a great deal of the emotional process before you even know a split is imminent. (He or she may also have stashed money or other assets, too, and done some financial housekeeping as well as emotional fine-tuning.)

If you find that you are unable to emotionally detach yourself from your anger, discuss with your attorney whether there is a way to delay making decisions concerning your financial status. (Certainly, this rule applies to custody decisions also!) You do not want to hold up the process indefinitely; however, taking a needed break may make better sense than acting rashly.

DON'T LET YOUR EMOTIONS GET IN THE WAY

A marital therapist stated, "Generally, the number one feeling that rules when divorce is impending is abandonment or betrayal.

People feel emotionally abused, too. Too often, when you want to get back at your partner, you do it economically. You may feel that you were in the marriage for the long haul, and when you find out it is over, you want revenge or punishment. And that gets translated into a desire for dollars and cents." The therapist's recommendation: "Get a grip on your emotions. You can't let fears or guilt or misplaced anger get in your way. That can end up costing you more in legal fees than you get in your settlement."

Remember: Your economic security is on the line.

A VIEW FROM THE BENCH

A Southwestern judge suggests a good approach to divorce. Do a self-examination. Identify your emotions so you can get a clearer picture of who you are. It will also help you understand why you may be fighting over a piece of property that really won't help you get the best business deal.

Money only renders the already significant differences between the sexes more glaring, and nowhere is this truer than in divorce. Whereas men often use conflict as a means of connecting with others, many women will go to any length to avoid conflict. Women tend to use cooperation and talking as a tool for working out their difficulties.

Don't let your emotions—specifically your desire to avoid hostility and other painful feelings—get in the way of fighting for what you deserve. Women tend to avoid hostility and overt anger; generally, wives are more willing than husbands to compromise for the sake of a relationship. Often, women in divorce negotiations avoid conflict for the sake of ending the relationship with as little face-to-face confrontation with their soon-to-be ex. But in the divorce arena, such women can lose financially because their fear of anger and dislike of hostility trumps their desire for financial security. Women often come away from divorce with a much diminished lifestyle. Whether you are male or female, not fighting for your fair share is easier than being aggressive and standing up for what you deserve. The problem is that not fighting may leave you broke.

Carol was married for a short time. Her husband, Sam, had a job that required him to do a lot of out-of-town travel. Carol was unhappy and lonely and had an affair with a co-worker. When she decided that she wanted out of the marriage, she confessed to Sam that she was having an affair. Sam was furious. He knew Carol loved the house they had bought together. She spent much of the time while he was traveling fixing up the house, adding a new family room, planting a garden, and landscaping a large backyard.

Sam decided to relocate, and he forced Carol to put the house up for sale and split the proceeds fifty-fifty, even though much of the appreciation in the value of the house was due solely to Carol's hard work. Carol, overwhelmed with guilt over the breakup, caved in and put the house up for sale rather than attempting to buy out Sam's share of the house and fight for her contribution, despite the fact that she would have been able to pay the mortgage payments and the upkeep of the house on her salary.

Carol's emotions got in the way of the business deal. She didn't do her economic homework. Instead, she allowed Sam's anger and her own guilt to overwhelm her.

Both men and women fall into the trap of giving away more than they should. As with Carol, this may occur out of guilt. At some point in the divorce process, my clients will declare that because the marriage has failed, they have failed, and they should pay for that failure. Men are more likely to want to "absolve" themselves of their supposed failure by giving away more financially to make up for this failing. When a man's earning capacity far exceeds his wife's, it may seem easier to throw money at a problem to work it out.

If a husband wants to provide generously for his wife and does so knowingly, that's fine. However, I have heard men complain ten years after their divorce that they should have thought twice because they acted out of guilt rather than generosity.

Dan and his wife were young and had no children. When divorce arose, his psychologist recommended that Dan get on with his life and get out of his marriage with as few emotional scars as possible. His lawyer pushed him not to give in and to fight a little harder to keep what was rightfully his. Dan decided not to fight, and he gave in on all the assets he considered "small things." He walked out of the marriage, leaving the house and everything in it.

Dan's wife didn't have a job at the time, and he felt sorry for her. He figured that as the major breadwinner, he should at least set her up at parting. Dan had a second objective: to walk away from the marriage without dealing with the pain. "There's a tendency for men to blow off stuff," he said. "It's a way to not deal with the pain." Facing a second divorce, Dan's resolve was strong. He didn't want to be hard-nosed, but he knew he could not afford to walk away without getting what was fair. One woman in the same situation echoed Dan's feeling about his first divorce: "You have got to deal with the emotional pain while you are going through the process, or it will haunt you later." It also may cost you a lot of money and property.

Both parties in a divorce usually end up with less than they need to live comfortably. You cannot afford to give up any part of your fair share merely because you are afraid of being yelled at. Conversely, you can't afford to give up too much because you feel guilty and just want to get it over with with the least amount of hassle. Doing what is least painful at the time rather than what is necessary can be costly in the end.

A VIEW FROM THE BENCH

One judge from the Midwest believes that if you are not in touch with your emotions and understand how they affect your judgment, you can't be rational—and you need to be rational when you are splitting property. She believes that many people harm themselves (as well as irritate judges) because they react in an emotional manner and don't argue reasoned positions. What irritates her most is people's failure to take responsibility for their part of the problem. As an example she cited women who take on the role of victim. This stance, says the judge, is a form of manipulative power. She detests when people feel that, as victims, they have paid their dues and now deserve everything—all the property and no debt. She made two suggestions:

1. *Ask yourself, "What is my contribution toward this problem?" No one is without fault. What does realizing this get you? My guess is that it lets you see things in a proper perspective and will enable you to make better decisions.*

2. *Get in touch with your emotions so you understand what is motivating you.*

In a divorce, each party feels wronged. This emotion at the bargaining table prevents you from seeing things clearly and reaching a good property division. Self-pity and victimization too often lead to a path of revenge, a "scorched Earth" policy in which you become fixated on grabbing everything you can to get back at your spouse.

In the eyes of the law, however, splitting property has little to do with revenge. In fact, in many states, the notion of fault does not enter into the equation of who gets what.

Unfortunately, money can represent power, control, or love itself.

When it comes to divorce, learn what money means to you. Determining what you value and why will help you examine your approach to the division of your marital property. What is motivating you to fight over a wedding present? Why do you want to keep the marital home if you can't afford to? Why don't you want to get your spouse's pension valued? Why are you fighting to keep the silverware when you could sell it, invest some of the money, and use the rest to pay off debt? Whatever your emotional attachments to certain things you jointly own, you have to work out your feelings. Don't blindly fight for objects it is not in your economic interest to keep.

Marriage merges two people with different backgrounds and belief systems into one unit, each bringing their own "baggage" into the new relationship. Often differing beliefs can separate rather than unite. Differing views may also prompt us to place too much weight or value on things that are not important. One judge from the West said that when marriages fail, people expect judges to come in and rearrange reality. "During the course of our lives," she states, "we develop strong beliefs. Many of them often go unexamined." To get at personal belief systems, this judge will often ask individuals before her to tell her all about their families. Were their parents divorced? If so, how old were they when they divorced? We do what our families taught us by their actions. Some of us grew up scrimping every penny. Others may have grown up in households where they lacked nothing.

Judges, lawyers, and therapists tell the same stories. Most couples displace their anger at one another by fighting over material objects or, worse, their children. Clashes of belief systems often find expression in the odd ways people treat certain items in a marital estate. They begin to obsess over objects that had little value for them before but that now, in the light of divorce, take on exaggerated (and often absurd) significance.

During divorce, you may obsess over not getting a certain piece of furniture a relative gave you as a wedding present when you should be focusing on the complete financial settlement and what you will have to live on. You may decide you can't sell the house you have spent so many years redecorating and raising your children in when you really should be focusing on whether you will have enough money after the divorce to afford the upkeep of the house.

Such obsessions usually are a waste of time, and they can decrease your final share of the marriage estate.

The antidote is to get ahold of your emotions. Examine what you *really* find valuable, and keep focused on the ultimate settlement—not revenge, not obsessions—the final deal.

IT'S A MATTER OF TRUST

Sex and money are often the catalysts to divorce because they get at the core issue of trust between partners. Shattered trust is an emotionally charged issue, but emotions cannot be allowed to spill over into the business deal.

Clients have come to see me after a spouse has confessed that they are contemplating bankruptcy because they owe substantial debts. Such bankruptcies often occur in a business situation, often when a spouse, as sole owner of the business, has 100 percent control of the money. Sometimes a disaster can start seemingly innocently. The business owner, as a spouse, short one payroll, borrows money to meet it—just this once. The next pay period rolls around, and more money is borrowed on the line of credit. Some spouses have even co-signed notes with their partners without understanding the financial consequences. (One educated professional felt she trusted her spouse enough to co-sign whatever he placed in front of her. When her spouse declared bankruptcy after their divorce, she was left paying the bills.) Who ultimately will bear responsibility for those bills will determine the quality of future lifestyles.

Sally was a great mom, a terrific teacher, and a coach for after-school sports. Her husband, Jim, ran a successful clothing business. The business started small but very quickly expanded to a number of locations. Jim bought Sally a new SUV and expensive jewelry, and he surprised her with some lavish vacations. Jim was financing these luxuries with money he should have used to pay taxes. When the taxing authorities caught up with Jim, Sally had gotten quite used to a fine standard of living. When a tax delinquency notice came in the mail, Sally confronted Jim. Jim promised that he would be responsible and start paying down the debt. Jim couldn't reform. He continued funding their lifestyle with his tax money because he was too ashamed to admit that he couldn't afford such luxuries any other way. Sally refused to face reality and see that her lifestyle couldn't continue unless she cut back. Sally also found herself attracted to the male soccer coach, her counterpart for the boy's team, and started a new relationship.

One year later, when Sally discovered that the tax bill was larger, she wanted out of the marriage. She thought she would just start a new life with her new friend. She decided divorce was the only option for her.

Jim wanted to save the marriage. However, he was crushed when he found out about Sally's new relationship. Jim faced bankruptcy. He decided that wasn't the route he wanted to take. Instead, Jim was faced with crushing debt. He was angry at Sally and felt she betrayed him with her affair. Sally, however, felt no guilt. She went after all their pensions and the marital home. Sally wanted the material possessions, and she got them. Jim was unable to let go of his shame. He gave in and gave Sally all the assets and none of the debt. Sally was lucky; she had not co-signed any notes, and she was not personally liable for the tax debt. Jim was saddled with hefty bills. He regretted that his shame prevented him from admitting to Sally that he was getting deeper into debt. A few years later he was still bitter and angry that he worked twelve-hour days six days a week to keep afloat. He recognized too late that Sally bore some fault for the relationship failing. He didn't cut a good business deal.

The bottom line is: Focus on finances. Don't get blindsided by hatred, inattention, anger, or revenge. You may feel cheated, abandoned, furious, and many other emotions, but you should put all this emotional energy into getting your full and complete financial picture. If you know all your individual and collective assets, you can cut your financial losses and be more in control of your life at a time when you feel most vulnerable and least able to cope. Controlling your emotions can translate into cutting your best financial deal.

Chapter Two

THE MARITAL ESTATE

You can't get your fair share of the marital estate unless you know what property is part of the marital estate. You need to be able to identify and list all of your property or you will lose the opportunity to fight for it.

YOURS, MINE, OURS . . . MINE!

Marriage is a partnership. When you start a partnership or a business you usually draw up a partnership agreement detailing how the property will be split in the event of a dissolution of the partnership. Marriages in which the parties have drawn up prenuptial or postnuptial agreements often can be dissolved similar to the way business partnerships can. Without a prenuptial or postnuptial agreement, the laws governing divorce in your state will determine how your possessions will be split and the percentage of the assets you will walk away with unless you and your former partner can work out an agreement.

A VIEW FROM THE BENCH

A Judge from the Southwest says, you need a basic understanding of the law. Then you need to properly inventory and classify your property.

INVENTORY YOUR PROPERTY

Before figuring out how you will divide your property, you must make a complete list of what you own. The list should include all the property you and your partner have acquired during your marriage, property you brought into the marriage, and any separate property you have received or purchased after your separation. (Property purchased before your marriage generally is not included in the marital estate although the appreciation on that property may be. Property acquired after separation is probably not included in the marital estate unless it is property purchased with money from the marriage or is an exchange for property you owned jointly during the marriage. Check with a lawyer to determine how specific property is treated in your state.)

A thorough list will include the following:

- *Any joint accounts. List all accounts, including the name of the bank or other financial institution, the type of account (savings, checking, money market, credit union), and the balance in each account. Make photocopies of all monthly or quarterly statements as they come in for each account.*

It is essential that you get account numbers and any other identifying information for bank accounts and any other accounts, including stocks, bonds, pensions, and insurance policies.

- *All stocks, bonds, mutual funds, and certificates of deposits you may jointly and separately own. Again, include all names and numbers on the accounts, if applicable. Make copies of any and all monthly or quarterly statements.*

- *Life insurance policies. Get copies of the policies if you can. Find out whether they are whole life policies or term. Call your insurance agent if you have questions.*

- *All real estate you own individually or jointly. This list should include your primary residence and any vacation homes or investment properties. Also, find out if there are any liens or judgments against the property. Note if there are any mortgages. If you can, find out what real estate is selling for near properties you own.*

- *All cars, trucks, and other motor vehicles or motorcycles you own. List the make, model, and year. Consult the Blue Book to determine the present value of these vehicles.*

- *All the furniture in all your homes.*

- *Valuable art, antiques, silver, or heirlooms separate from the above.*

- *Jewelry.*

- *Boats, airplanes, or recreational vehicles.*

- *Any collections you may have. For example, if you collect stamps or coins, list the type, content, and market value (you may need to consult philatelists, numismatics, or other experts). The more specific the list, the better off you will be and the less work a lawyer will need to do if you have to request discovery—the legal route to find out what you and/or your spouse own.*

- *All retirement or pension plans. This list will include any traditional or Roth IRAs, Keogh plans, pensions, and profit sharing plans (401[k]s).*

- *Stock options and any employee stock ownership plans.*

- *Annuities.*

- *All businesses you own or in which you have an ownership interest.*

- *Contents of any safe-deposit boxes. It is best to videotape or take pictures of everything in the box in case your spouse visits the box and removes any of the contents. If anything is missing, you will be able to document it.*

- *Any personal injury lawsuits.*

- *Inheritances.*

- *Professional licenses.*

- *Any debts owed to you or your spouse.*

- *Copyrights, royalties, or patents.*

You will also need to make a list of all debts you and your spouse may owe. Specifically list the following:

- *All loans. This includes any money from any financial lending institution, including loans for motor vehicles, boats, motorcycles, or any other assets you have financed rather than purchased outright. Include loans against your retirement plans or brokerage accounts. You may need to call your broker or the administrator of your retirement plan to get this information.*

- *All your credit cards and the account numbers. Keep a list of all the account balances. Again, copy all the statements that come in.*

CLASSIFY YOUR REAL ESTATE AND PERSONAL PROPERTY

You need to review your inventory of items. With that list in hand, answer the following questions:

- *What property did you buy or own before the marriage? Review your inventory of items and identify which ones you owned prior to marriage.*

- *What property did your spouse own before the marriage?*

- *What property did you and your spouse purchase together?*

- *What property did you receive as gifts? Were those gifts given to one spouse individually or to both of you?*

Before you can figure out what property is marital property, you need to divide the property into separately owned property and jointly owned. Not all the property will fit neatly into one category or the other. If you have a problem identifying an item, put a question mark next to it.

In the case of property that you brought into the marriage but made improvements or additions to while you were married, the property may fall into a hybrid category. Remember that property owned separately may have increased in value during your marriage. The amount of increase or the appreciation of that separate property is generally considered joint marital property when figuring out the division.

You may have married young and come into the marriage with no money or assets. Or you might have waited until you were older before getting married. In that case, you may already own your own furnished apartment, house, or condo. But suppose your spouse moves in after the wedding and you two live in the house. You may have jointly fixed up the house, put on a new roof, or built a new kitchen, or bought paintings, additional furnishings, and other upgrades for your home. Under these circumstances, you need to determine what part of the house is considered marital property, which part is separate property, and who gets credit for what. These are some of the issues in a property division.

Equally important: Some couples finance a home or borrow money from a line of credit and use the house for collateral or as security for the loan. Mortgages and lines of credit are classified as debt. If the marriage dissolves, the question becomes: Who is responsible for paying the debts?

Separate Property

Certain types of property are considered separate property or property belonging to only one person in the marriage.

The division of separate property and jointly owned property may be treated differently when dividing property. You need to check the rules in your state. (See the "Equitable Distribution" and "Community Property" sections later in this chapter.)

Separate property can include the following:

- *Money you inherit during your marriage that you keep in a separate account under your name alone and do not put it into a joint account.*

- *Any gifts given to you alone either before or during the marriage.*

- *Any property you bring into the marriage—property you owned before you got married.*

- *Property you acquire after separation, as long as it is not purchased with money from the marriage or is not an exchange for property you owned jointly during the marriage.*

- *In community property states, any property you accumulate during your marriage that comes from any earnings you received before you got married is considered separate property. One example is a pension that might have vested before you got married. Another example is any asset you accumulate during your marriage that comes from or is paid for with money that you had before you got married. For example, if you saved money before you got married and then used it to buy investment property during the marriage, the property may be separate property.*

Joint Property

With some exceptions, property you and your spouse acquired during your marriage is joint property. For example, a house a couple purchases while married may be considered joint property. If property bought before marriage appreciated in value during your marriage, the amount of that appreciation may be considered joint property. For example, if you purchased a home before you got married and it goes up in value while you are married, the increase in value may be considered joint property.

If you have taken separate property and mingled it into joint property, make certain to get all the documentation to help you prove that the property once was separate. Next, get proof of the amount of separate property that was commingled. Such documentation does not guarantee you will get credit for the money, but it gives you a better shot at it.

One of the stickiest problems in divorce occurs when one spouse merges separate property into a joint asset. For example, if one spouse buys a house before marriage, sells it during marriage, then takes the money and puts it into a house purchased jointly, in many states the money put into the joint home would be considered a gift to the marriage and, therefore, joint property.

Certain states will sometimes—but not always—give full or partial credit to the spouse who "gifted" the money. To get credit for the money in this situation, it is essential that you document the amount of money, where it came from, and the joint property it was used to purchase. I often advise clients to get copies of their bank statements that reflect the amount of money withdrawn from their separate bank account and that was deposited into a joint account or delivered to the mortgage company to cover the down payment of a jointly purchased home. You cannot hear this advice enough because it does bear repeating: **Document, document, document!**

Now that you have classified and inventoried all your property and debt, you need to find out whether you live in a community property state or an equitable distribution state.

The following states are community property states: Arizona, California, Idaho, Louisiana, Nevada, New Mexico, Texas, Washington, and Wisconsin. All other states generally apply the principles of equitable distribution. Rules vary state to state, but you must at least understand the basics.

EQUITABLE DISTRIBUTION

In most states, the courts take the view that all joint property should be equitably or fairly divided when you decide to split. But the word *equitable* may turn out to be anything but what you might expect. The one truism about divorce is that it is generally anything but fair!

Usually judges start with the proposition that equitable distribution is a fifty-fifty split of joint property and may also include a fifty-fifty split of appreciation during marriage of any separate property. One spouse may get more than 50 percent if the court finds a good reason for it. Each state has laws that provide factors within which a court or other fact-finder determines what percentage of the property is reasonable or equitable for each party to receive. These factors vary from state to state.

However, fact-finders in all states generally will ask many of the same kinds of questions to decide how to divide marital assets fairly. So be prepared: Have ready and documentable answers for the following questions.

Factors Often Considered in Equitable Distribution

- *How long were you married?*

- *How old are you and your spouse?*

- *Are you in good health?*

- *How much do you and your spouse earn and, if you are not now working, what are you capable of earning?*

- *How much is each of you likely to earn in the future?*

- *What is your education and/or your past work history?*

- *What are the sources of income both earned and unearned?*

- *What assets or property have you received or acquired separately during the marriage, and what is that property worth?*

- *How have you and your spouse each contributed to the marriage?*

- *Has one party dissipated or squandered any of the marital assets?*

- *Does one party in the marriage have any special needs?*

- *What is your standard of living?*

- *What are your liabilities and debts?*

- *Do you or your spouse have a professional degree, such as a law degree or medical practice? Did you support your spouse while he or she was going through school to get the degree? (Different states place varying emphasis on this question, so consult an attorney to find out if this question applies in your state.)*

Each of these factors may be weighed differently. Again, if you view your marriage as a partnership, you'd expect that the longer you were married and the more time you have invested, the greater the return will be. It doesn't always work out that clearly. You must weigh all the above factors.

Courts will pay great attention to the duration of the marriage. Generally, a marriage lasting two years is seen much differently from one lasting twenty. Most jurisdictions look at marriages of fifteen to twenty years and beyond as long-term marriages.

The longer spouses are married, the more defined their roles might be. For example, if two people are married for twenty years and have children, one partner might have stayed at home to take a greater part in raising the children. If both of you worked outside the home, one partner may have been the primary breadwinner while the other partner had more responsibilities for the household. Or both parties may have shared equally in household responsibilities and in earning money. In determining the divorce settlement, the court must come up with a dollar figure representing each of your contributions.

There are often extenuating circumstances that might affect your ability to contribute to the partnership. You may suffer a debilitating illness during the marriage or you may discover that you have a degenerative illness such as multiple sclerosis or Parkinson's disease. These illnesses may not affect your earning capacity or your ability to care for children or spouse now, but they may affect your earning ability in the future.

Consider the following scenario:

Ted and Carol met in college and have been married for more than thirty years. Carol worked in an accounting company for a few years while Ted completed a master's in business administration.

Ted started in a career-track program at a national department store. Carol and Ted wanted to start a family while the two of them were still young, and when Carol became pregnant she stopped working. Ted and Carol had three children in quick succession. Carol stayed at home and raised the kids while Ted opened his own retail store. One day, when all the children were finally out of the house and Carol was easing into empty nesting, Ted came home and announced that he no longer wanted to be married.

Carol is now in her mid-fifties. She had worked only a short period of time during the marriage. They enjoyed a modest lifestyle. Every penny was usually spent on the children's schooling and activities. Although she remains as active as possible, Carol suffers from arthritis and severe asthma. She was looking forward to retiring early with her husband and worries that she has no marketable skills.

Although Carol helped Ted in the store during holidays and other busy times, she is not able to stand on her feet all day long selling clothing or any other items. She also helped Ted with some basic bookkeeping, but her skills are rather rudimentary. She had taken many business courses and some accounting courses in college, but here again, her skills are quite outdated. She is not computer-literate, and she failed the course she took on computers. Ted did not primarily rely on Carol's minimal expertise in maintaining the books and records. In fact, he hired an accountant to prepare the tax returns and help with other financial matters.

Ted and Carol have a very nice home in the suburbs with a small mortgage and two cars. Ted has a small 401(k). Both use their joint credit cards liberally, so there are monthly bills that need to be paid.

Ted works six days a week. He has diabetes, which he controls through medication, but he was hospitalized once for treatment for his diabetes. He would like to retire earlier rather than later and spend time with his new girlfriend—a nurse he met when he was hospitalized.

Both Ted and Carol were hoping for an early retirement during which, they both understood, they would have a very modest standard of living. Carol had hoped they would grow old together. Ted had originally planned on the same thing. However, spending most of his time working in the store to pay family bills and the rest of the time doing family activities, Ted grew apart from Carol. He wants to start a new life with his girlfriend.

Any fact-finder would have to consider the following questions in order to determine an equitable split of Carol and Ted's property:

- *What was Carol's contribution to the marriage?*

  1. As homemaker?

  2. As a help in the business?

- *How do Carol's bookkeeping skills translate into a future earning capacity?*

- *Will Carol's health offset her ability to earn a living?*

- *After thirty years of marriage, can Carol expect alimony as well as a percentage of property? If yes, for what length of time?*

- *Will's Carol's age affect the property division?*

- *What is the value of all the assets (house, pension, cars, business)?*

- *Is Carol entitled to any part of Ted's pension?*

- *Should Ted and Carol sell the house and split the proceeds, or should Carol keep the house and Ted get his pension or the business?*

- *How does Ted's health affect the property division?*

- *Who pays the debts?*

After considering the answers to these questions, a fact-finder will decide how to divide the property. Carol may receive 60 percent of the property and Ted 40 percent. Or Carol may receive 50 percent or 55 percent of the property and receive alimony for a period of time. Unfortunately, the skill of a lawyer may make a difference in the percentages received. There are no hard-and-fast rules.

Dividing the property can be very complicated, with many variables factoring into the decision.

COMMUNITY PROPERTY

The community property concept follows the view that marriage is an equal partnership and that all the property acquired during the marriage should be split fifty-fifty. All wages and income, as well as all property and debt, are considered community property. Separate property generally retains its classification, and the spouse who owns it generally gets to keep it.

There are some exceptions, however. If you bring separate property into the marriage and keep it separate during the marriage, it will remain your separate property. But beware of exceptions in some states. For example, in Texas, if you buy a house one month before your marriage and title it in your name alone but you live in the house along with your spouse for twenty-five years and use money you both earned to pay for the mortgage and the upkeep of the house, the law will take the joint contribution into consideration and rule that part of the home is, indeed, marital property. The law allows both parties in the partnership to benefit from the ownership of the house. This concept tries to address the anomalies in the law that state that if you come into the marriage with an asset titled in your name alone but both parties contribute to the asset, then both should enjoy the benefits of the ownership if you split up.

Some community property states leave wiggle room to consider other factors when dividing the property. Generally, judges will exercise discretion to vary the split from a straight fifty-fifty when there is some compelling or significant factor, for example, if there is a significant health issue that needs to be factored in. In Ted and Carol's case, if either's health became disabling and one or the other was unable to work, the court might consider giving a greater percentage of the assets to the spouse who was disabled. Other factors that may affect the percentage of the property division are a major difference in earning capacity between the spouses; the size of separate estates, if any; the length of the marriage; and one spouse's squandering assets.

If you own separate property that generates income during the marriage, the income may be considered part of the community property. For example, if you separately own a duplex and rent it out, the income you receive from the property may be considered part of the community property. But property appreciation may be exempt. If the value of the duplex was to increase during the marriage (you bought it for $75,000 but it is worth $100,000 when you divorce), the increase in value (or the $25,000) may not be considered part of the community property. To be safe, check with a lawyer in your state.

Another example of how rules can be bent is if one partner takes money that belongs to the community property and pays off a separate debt, then the community property will be paid back that amount when the parties split.

If one partner has an accident during the marriage, sues, and receives a personal injury award, the award may be considered part of the community property if the injured party was pursuing an activity that was part of the marriage. For example, if you were driving your children to an extracurricular activity and were rear-ended, the money you receive from the lawsuit may be considered part of community property. Be sure to check the laws in your state.

> *Begin by making lists of everything you and your spouse own. Be sure to include all the identifying numbers and other information to help locate these accounts and determine what they might be worth. Classify the property. Make a list of any and all outstanding debt. Find out if you live in a community property state or an equitable distribution state.*
>
> *Before you know what you are eligible to receive in a divorce settlement, you need to accurately catalog all your separate and joint assets. Also remember to check with the laws in your state if community property or equitable distribution will apply.*
>
> *The following chart may help you with your paperwork.*

Husband

Social Security number

Birthdate

Wife

Social Security number

Birthdate

ASSETS

Indicate whether the property is owned jointly, separately, or for the benefit of children. For example: husband (H), wife (W), or for the benefit of children (C). Also indicate whether any assets were received by inheritance (I), given as a gift before or during marriage (G), or was owned before marriage (P).

REAL ESTATE

Type of property
(marital home, vacation home, rental property)

Address of property

Date of purchase

Original cost

Current market value

Mortgage/balance owed

List any liens of judgments against the property.

(If purchased prior to marriage, list the increase or decrease in value since the date of marriage.)

Retirement

Name/type of plan

Account number

Value

Date

Life Insurance

Type

Name of company

Policy number

(Indicate face value, cash surrender value, and current beneficiaries.)

Cars

Make/model/year

Loan outstanding

Current value

Savings Accounts

Name of institution/number

Type of account

Balance

Checking Accounts

Name of institution

Type of account

Balance

Securities

Name of company

Number of shares

Value

Bonds
Indentifying information

Value

Mutual fund
    Indentifying information

Options
    Identifying information

    When acquired

Certificates of deposit
    Identifying information

    Amount

Cash
    Amount

Money-market funds
    Identifying information

    Amount

Annuities
    Identifying information

    Amount

Trust
    Identifying information

    Amount

Business Interests

List owners, including the percentage of ownership and all positions held in the company.

_____

Employment Termination Benefits

List workers' compensation claims and awards as well as any severance pay.

_____

Retirement/Pension Plans

Type

Date of vesting

Employee contribution

_____

Household Property and Other Personal Property

List all furnishings in any and all houses; all artwork, antiques, jewelry, collections, boats, airplanes, or horses; and any other property owned by you or your spouse.

_____

Patents, Copyrights, Inventions, Royalties

Have you disposed of any assets valued at $500 or more within the last year? If so, list. Do you currently have any lawsuits pending in this or any other state? If yes, list the name and number of the suit. Have you ever filed for bankruptcy? If so, list all details.

Liabilities

Creditor's name

Account number

Amount

Monthly payments

Who pays?

Date incurred

Date due

List any and all credit cards, store charges, student loans, bank loans, home-equity loans, mortgages, liens and judgments, loans against retirement and brokerage accounts, personal loans, outstanding taxes owed, and any and all other outstanding debts.

Chapter Three

UNDERSTANDING EVERYDAY FINANCES

Most states require you to fill out a form in which you list all the income both you and your spouse receive from all sources and all the debts you and your spouse owe. You need to assemble this information early in the divorce process for two reasons:

1. *Your lawyer, mediator, or judge will require it.*

2. *You need to get a clear picture of your income and debts so you can determine how much you'll need to live after divorce.*

> ### A VIEW FROM THE BENCH
>
> A judge from the Southeast offers the following advice: Be practical. Get all the facts and figures you need to make an educated decision about how much to settle for. One of the most important steps that a person going through a divorce must take seriously is filling out the financial affidavit of income, expenses, and liabilities.

Although this information doesn't take the place of a financial adviser, you must know which forms you need to copy and take to a lawyer, accountant, or other expert to find out how much money is coming in, how much money is going out, and to whom you owe any money.

WHAT IS INCOME?

To get a good settlement, including a fair property division and monthly support, you need to know how much income you and your spouse produce.

Although courts take other factors into consideration, they generally base awards of child support and spousal support or maintenance on the amount of monthly income you and your spouse earn as well as any other income either of you may have.

Income can include any of the following:

- *Salary, wages, and tips*

- *Unemployment benefits or disability benefits*

- *Profits from any and all businesses*

- *Unemployment benefits*

- *Rents*

- *Commissions*

- *Dividends on stocks and mutual funds*

- *Interest income from any source*

- *Social Security benefits*

- *Pension benefits*

- *Royalties and advances against royalties*

- *Bonuses (including signing bonuses, yearly bonuses, commissions on sales, or incentive bonuses)*

- *Awards and prizes from any source*

- *Gifts*

- *Inheritances (depending on your state)*

- *Payment for jury duty*

Although these are some of the more common and tangible sources of income, there are other sources of income that are harder to determine and may be more difficult to evaluate. Consider this:

Tom worked for XYZ computer company as a salesperson for ten years. Because Tom needed to travel a few hundred miles a week, XYZ leased a new Mercedes for Tom every three years. In addition, XYZ matched Tom's monthly contributions to his pension plan. They paid for his health coverage for his spouse and two children. Because Tom's job required him to be on the road for a few weeks at a time, XYZ paid all his living expenses, including meals, gas mileage, cellular phone bills, and any fees for health clubs he used when the hotels did not include those fees in the package. (XYZ felt that to be mentally fit you need to be physically fit.) XYZ liked their employees to keep current on all the latest computer technology, so they encouraged employees to take courses at the local community college. Once employees were trained enough to enter XYZ's management program, the company paid for all courses at other universities with degree programs. They footed the bill for these expenses. They also provided a day-care center for their employees at minimal cost.

Tom's paystubs did not reflect these additional "perks" or the dollar amount these benefits represented. But such extras, or at least a portion of them, may be considered income in some states. When courts determine how much Tom should pay for child support, alimony, or spousal maintenance, these perks may be converted to dollar amounts and added to the evaluation of Tom's base income. The court or mediator would ask: How much money would Tom have to pay for these benefits if the company did not pay for them? How much does it cost a month to lease his car? How much are the fees for his health club? How much is the tuition for the courses? How much does day care cost? Once a dollar amount is determined, it may be considered as additional income for Tom; the rationale being that Tom is getting personal benefits he might have otherwise received in cash payments.

When determining your spouse's income, then, look for extras like these that don't show up as visibly as wages. You may discover that your spouse is receiving benefits in addition to a base salary. How can you uncover these "extras"? Make a list of everything your spouse receives from the company. What activities are paid for by the company? Who pays telephone or cell phone bills? Does your spouse have use of a company car? Does the employer foot the bills for vacations? What about meals? You may want to ask your lawyer for help. There may even be times when you may want to use a private investigator. You might also need advice from an accountant or financial adviser.

You can find out about perks by using certain documents. The most important document you need to figure out whether or not your spouse may have "additional" income is a tax return. If your spouse owns a business, is a partner in a business, or is self-employed, you will need business tax returns as well as individual returns. It might be necessary to hire an accountant or a forensic accountant to help you determine the correct dollar amount of all the income. An attorney may be able to advise you which experts would be helpful.

Now let's consider the documents you must obtain to get all the necessary information to determine income. There are a range of them—and they aren't easy for the nonexpert to understand. However, you do not need to be able to read and understand these tax returns; your lawyer or financial adviser can help you do that. If you can or want to learn how, so much the better. But even the most "tax-challenged" spouse must gather all the information possible. The following is a list of tax documents you may need to get a more accurate picture of income:

- *Individual tax returns. These are the yearly returns that should be filed every April 15.*

- *Partnership tax returns. Schedule K-1 is a partner's share of income from a partnership and will detail any of the extra perks or fringe benefits a partner may receive, such as entertainment costs, travel and expenses, and club fees.*

- *If the business is not a corporation, look for the Schedule C portion of the individual tax return. Schedule C details any profit or loss from a business.*

- *If you are dealing with income from a farm, you will need Schedule F.*

- *Schedule L may indicate any loans made to shareholders that may also be part of income disguised as a loan. If your spouse is a principal owner of a business, you might want to check to see if money classified as a "loan" was given to your spouse. Sometimes loans are used as a way to manipulate the amount of personal income received when a divorce proceeding is occurring.*

- *Schedule M-1 may disclose income recorded in financial records but not appearing on tax returns, for example tax-exempt interest.*

Again, you may not be able to decipher the information on these returns by yourself. You should at least recognize that you will need to get copies of as many of these documents as are relevant. If you are unable to obtain these yourself, your lawyer can always request that your spouse's lawyer supply you with this information. (Remember: It is always less expensive to get information yourself without your lawyer's, accountant's, or other expert's help. Another advantage of obtaining information without involving lawyers and having to get formal "discovery" of documents is that any documents you get without a formal request can help determine whether information obtained later in formal discovery is accurate and complete. Having documentation in hand is a good test of your spouse's honesty!)

If you or your spouse is working for a business, other documents will be helpful in determining the income of the business and the value of the business. (This will be discussed more fully in Chapter Seven on business valuation.) The following documents are helpful:

- *Credit card statements, especially if your spouse has a separate credit card used solely for business expenses.*

- *Partnership agreements. Such documents will reveal what percentage a partner has in a business, as well as possible perks.*

- *Shareholder agreements.*

- *Buy/sell agreements. This document reveals how much the partnership is willing to pay the partner for his share of the business should the partnership have to buy him or her out, as well as other relevant information.*

- *Applications for loans. Such documents often reveal salaries, assets, and debts.*

- *Employment contracts. These should spell out the terms of employment, including any and all sources of income.*

- *Financial statements. These should include all income received and all assets owned.*

- *Any employee manuals (from companies your spouse works or has worked for) that might describe benefits to employees.*

These documents may contain valuable income information. Methodically gather all this information so you can figure out how much your spouse really earns and how much a business may be worth.

HOW MUCH DO WE SPEND?

The next big question is: How much money does it take for me to live? That question may involve you alone, or it might also take into account the needs of children. The bottom line is that running a household should be treated the same as running a business. No business would survive without a complete accounting of all monies going in and all monies going out. Just as every successful business has a business plan, every successful divorce takes planning ahead.

A VIEW FROM THE BENCH

One judge from the Midwest says that it continually amazes her that people never anticipate what it costs to maintain two households, especially when most people live from paycheck to paycheck. In the beginning of her hearings, she goes through a budget with both parties. She believes that both spouses need to figure out how much it costs to run a single household. Then, you must determine the cost of running two houses. Before you split, work the numbers so you can plan ahead.

Often when you are a couple, you fail to notice all the money you pay to different companies and for other everyday living expenses. One judge from the Northeast states that the one given is that it definitely will cost a great deal more to run two households, so you need to start paying attention to what your money is being spent on.

How Much Does It Cost to Run Your Household?

Although there are computer programs available today that can help you determine your expenses, you don't need to be that technologically sophisticated to do so. Paper and pencil are all that is required to begin.

First, consider your housing costs. Most people either own or rent. If you rent, your first number should be the cost of your rental unit each month. If you own your home, write down how much you pay each month on your mortgage. Some mortgages include taxes and other fees in the monthly figure. Find out what costs are included in your mortgage, if any. List any monthly fees associated with your mortgage or any condominium or cooperative fees. Also list any real estate taxes not included in these figures.

Next, determine how much you pay each month for your utilities—gas bills, electric bills, water and sewer costs, telephone and fuel oil costs, if applicable. If you pay quarterly for these costs, divide the amount of your quarterly payment by four. If you do not keep the checkbook in your family, now is the time to obtain it and make a copy of your check register. This should list the amounts paid and to whom. If you can't get access to the checkbook and the account the checks are written on is a joint account, call the bank and order copies of the checks. For a fee, you should be able to get back checks or a list of checks, the amounts paid, and to whom. If all else fails, call the utility companies and get copies of your bills and accounts.

Detail any and all bills for maintenance on your home, whether for a broken hot water heater, a new roof, or maintenance or upgrades for your apartment. Receipts are always helpful. Again, if you paid by check or credit card, keep a copy of the statements.

Figure out all your other monthly expenses such as education costs, cable bills, and Internet accounts. Calculate your food bills by keeping your grocery receipts. Ditto for toiletries and incidentals at the drugstore.

If you own a car, keep a record of how much you pay for gas. Find out how much you pay for car insurance. If you pay for your insurance premiums yearly, divide that premium by twelve to get your monthly cost. And don't forget maintenance costs. If you pay to garage your car, add that expense. If you do not own a car, add your costs for public transportation or car rentals.

Your next category might be clothing. List your clothing bills separately from your children's. Include cleaning costs. Consider the types of clothing you need—jackets, sweaters, pants, suits, athletic wear, shoes, and whatever else you might buy for your lifestyle. Remember: In alimony and child support, the courts consider what your current standard of living is when determining how much money you should receive. If you do not accurately report what you spend, you will not give the court an accurate picture of your lifestyle.

Caution: One major mistake some separated couples make is to allow the spouse to go out and spend more money than usual. They do it to assuage their guilt over the demise of the relationship. If you try to atone this way and later must divorce, you may end up paying more in support because you will have allowed your spouse to artificially inflate your lifestyle!

A VIEW FROM THE BENCH

One judge from Pennsylvania suggests the following: Review every type of expenditure you and your spouse have made together. Don't overlook anything. List boats, motorcycles, furs and other expensive articles of clothing, jewelry, artwork, antiques, musical instruments, computers, stereo equipment, "guy gadgets," "girl necessities," and any other expensive possessions. If you are paying monthly bills for any of these items, include those payments in your list.

If you have taken vacations during your marriage, list the approximate cost of each. Get copies of credit card statements or checks written to cover these expenses. Again, you can figure out how much you spent yearly and divide by twelve to get your monthly cost.

Secure receipts for all child care costs. If you pay your baby-sitter in cash, bring receipts with you to the hearing. Compile all receipts and categorize them so you can prove your expenses if necessary.

I sometimes recommend to clients that they keep a daily log for at least one month of all the money they spend. This tends to be a good exercise as well as a wake-up call concerning how much money actually leaves their hands each month. One client actually remarked that he was unaware how much his daily cups of coffee and latté cost!

Another category of major expense is insurance. Whether it is life insurance, disability insurance, personal property insurance, car insurance, or any other insurance policy you may pay for, make certain that you account for every dollar spent. Again, if you do not pay the bills, you may need to do some investigative work. Call your insurance agent to find out the cost of your insurance premiums.

A major concern for both men and women today is health insurance. It costs a great deal, and couples go with whoever's coverage is best. Divorce may represent the end of your insurance coverage. I have actually had clients who did not want to divorce because their spouses had a good insurance policy with a prescription plan or other benefit that my clients were reluctant to give up. If you run the risk of losing insurance coverage because of your divorce, find out just how much the equivalent coverage would cost for you, your spouse, and your children.

There is a federal law, Consolidated Omnibus Budget Reconciliation Act of 1985, or COBRA, which allows you to continue being covered after divorce under whatever policy you were covered under before and carry that coverage for up to thirty-six months as long as your spouse works for an entity that employs twenty or more people. If your spouse's employer is smaller, you can always get single coverage in an HMO, traditional indemnity, or other plan. These options may cost more. It is necessary, however, to get all the information about your current coverage and whether or not you can continue it after the divorce. If you do your homework, you will be able to tell a master or judge what you expect it will cost for your health insurance in the future. Don't rely on your spouse to give you this information. Call your spouse's employer's personnel manager or the employee benefits officer to get the information yourself and ensure its accuracy.

If your spouse has dental and/or vision coverage, find out the details about these policies as well. If you have children, make certain you find out about orthodontia costs. If it is not included in any insurance coverage, it may be wise to include the cost of such coverage in your property settlement agreement.

The same goes for psychological coverage. Some insurance coverage provides for a limited number of visits for psychological help. One thing is certain: Most people seek the help of a therapist during this stressful time. If you have children and are divorcing, you may want to have your children speak with a neutral third party such as a counselor, social worker, or psychologist. Determine who will pay for any part of this expense not covered by insurance. Too many times one spouse just assumes the other will do the best thing for the child and help pay the bills. Often this is an incorrect assumption. Find out the cost of psychological coverage beforehand and include this cost on your expense sheet.

Also document tuition for school and extracurricular activities. (For more details see Chapter Twelve on child support.)

List any entertainment you regularly schedule: eating out, movies, books, magazine subscriptions, gym memberships, skating, or skiing. List any and all activities in which you generally engage. Keeping a log of your daily activities may help you remember all additional expenditures.

Again, if you are unfamiliar with your costs, begin to open all the financial statements as they come in the mail and make copies. Preplanning is always best. Educate yourself as to the cost of your daily life.

WHAT DO WE OWE AND TO WHOM?

One judge from the Southwest likes to pose this question to divorcing couples. He believes it's just as compelling as "What income do we have?" Too often, couples forget that it's not just "What's ours is mine," but also "What we owe is often the responsibility of both of us"—especially if both spouses have co-signed a note, home-equity loan, or mortgage, or hold joint credit cards or other joint responsibilities.

The problem with marital debt is that often when you co-sign a note or apply for a joint credit card, you are not just agreeing with your spouse to pay for a debt. You are binding yourself to a contract with a third party. Consider this:

John and Nancy jointly apply to XYZ electronic store for a store credit card. In essence, they agree that they will be jointly liable to pay for whatever purchases either of them makes from XYZ. John and Nancy are making a contract with XYZ that if either buys something from the store—for example, a CD player—that either one or the other will be responsible for paying for it. If John leaves the marriage and refuses to pay for the CD player, the store has a legal right to go after Nancy to get the money. When you apply for a joint credit card with which either party may make a purchase, the store can try to collect from either party to get their money. Even if John assured Nancy that he would pay for the CD player, when he skips town and refuses to pay for it, XYZ can collect from Nancy.

Divorcing couples can stipulate in the property settlement agreement which spouse is responsible for which debts. Remember, though, that a property settlement agreement is a contract between you and your soon-to-be-ex. A third party—such as a credit card company or the store in the earlier example—is not bound by the agreement. If one spouse agrees to pay for a debt after divorce and then defaults, a third party can then go after either spouse for payment of the debt. You may consider sending a copy of the applicable portion of your agreement to the third party; however, most creditors refuse to be bound to this. If your spouse assumes a debt, you can try to get a written release from liability from the creditor. This is the only way you can be assured that you will not be held responsible for paying the debt. Again, most third parties are reluctant to let you off the hook.

One of the best ways to work out debt is to do some planning before you separate. Just as you listed all your income, you need to list all your debts. If you own a home, the first creditor you can list is the mortgage company. Find out how much you presently owe on your mortgage. If you have any home-equity loans, list the name of the financial institution that lent the money and also list the account number and any other pertinent information concerning the loan. Are you making monthly car payments? If so, list the name of the finance company and the monthly payment as well as the number of payments you owe. As with all other financial matters concerning your divorce, you need to get as much specific information as you can. Make a list of all credit cards you hold both individually and jointly. Open and copy all statements or call the companies and find out how much is due on each card.

You may want to consider each taking out a new loan in separate names, paying off the joint debt, then each only bearing responsibility for the debt in your name alone.

What Happens If You Have No Assets—Just Debt?

Sometimes, the marital estate consists only of debt and no assets. If this is the case, you may want to consult a consumer credit counselor. You may need help consolidating your debts and coming up with a payment schedule. However, if your debts far exceed your assets and you are not able to pay off these debts, you may need to consider filing for bankruptcy. If both spouses file for bankruptcy, neither will be responsible for paying off the debts.

However, if one files for bankruptcy and the other does not, the one who does not file may end up on the hook for the joint debts. Before considering bankruptcy, review all the facts with a consumer counselor or bankruptcy lawyer.

A credit counselor can negotiate with your creditors to reduce the amount you owe, lower your interest rates, and get a monthly payment plan. If you owe money to many different companies, a counselor can juggle your payments for you.

Be aware that debt counselors sometimes charge a fee for their services. The creditor might pay a fee or sum of money to the agency. As with all your experts, make sure you know how much this service will cost you.

Questions to Ask a Debt Counselor

- *Do you charge fees for this service?*

- *What is the fee based on?*

- *Do you receive any money back from the creditors?*

- *Do you negotiate with creditors to compromise the outstanding amount of the debt?*

- *Do you provide services other than paying off debts?*

- *Do you provide financial counseling?*

The National Foundation of Consumer Credit Counseling Service, also known as The Consumer Credit Counseling Service (www.nfcc.org; 1-800-388-2227), a nonprofit association, can negotiate with credit card companies to help reduce your debt. They may also be able to help you come up with a budget you can live by. Each state has a different branch. Check with the agency to determine whether or not you will need to pay a nominal fee for this service.

If you do choose to use a for-profit counseling service, make inquiries to determine if they are legitimate. You might try contacting your local Better Business Bureau. If you use a disreputable company, you may lose the fee and still bear the responsibility for your debts.

In preparing for divorce, you absolutely must do your homework. Focus on your finances. If you need help gathering facts and figures, ask for it. You can't secure your financial future without the necessary information.

The following chart and budget may help to organize your monthly expenses.

GROSS MONTHLY INCOME

Salary, including wages and commissions (may include any of the following)

   Husband: Annual income   Wife: Annual income

Retirement
(income from any pension or profit-sharing plan)

Social Security benefits

Dividends or interest

Royalties

Rents

Annuities

Unemployment compensation

Workers' compensation

Disability

Expense account

Alimony

TOTAL GROSS INCOME

MONTHLY DEDUCTION

Federal income tax

State income tax

Local wage tax

Social Security taxes

Medicare taxes

Union and other mandatory dues

Credit union

Retirement
(indicate whether this deduction is mandatory or voluntary)

Savings plans of any type

Health insurance
(list company, type, and policy number)

Life insurance
(list company, type, and policy number)

Other insurance

Repayment of loans

TOTAL MONTHLY DEDUCTIONS

Note: Many states will only consider mandatory deductions such as taxes as qualifying as allowable deductions when determining your monthly income upon which your support obligations will be based.

TOTAL NET INCOME

BUDGET

Most states want you to fill out three different columns. One column includes the dollar amount you spend on yourself. The next column will include what you spend on your children. The next column is what your spouse may spend. You may only be able to fill out two of the three columns; however, when you and your spouse exchange budgets, you will have a more complete picture of the cost of running two households.

Please indicate what you spend monthly on each item.

	HUSBAND	WIFE	CHILD/REN
Mortgage or rent			
Real estate taxes			
Personal property taxes			
Utilities			
Gas			
Electric			
Fuel oil			
Telephone			
Water/sewer			
Repair and maintenance			
Insurance			
Homeowner's			
Car			
Life			
Accident			
Health			
Long-term care			

	HUSBAND	WIFE	CHILD/REN
Disability			
Umbrella / catastrophic			
Other			
Car			
Monthly payments			
Fuel/oil			
Repairs			
Insurance			
Transportation			
Bus			
Taxicabs			
Medical			
Doctor			
Dentist			
Orthodontist			
Hospital			
Medicine			

	HUSBAND	WIFE	CHILD/REN
Special needs			
Personal			
Food			
Laundry			
Dry cleaning			
Barber/hairdresser			
Clothing			
Shoes			
Magazines and newspapers			
Club memberships			
Gifts			
Donations			
Child care			
Day care			
Camps			
Travel			

	HUSBAND	WIFE	CHILD/REN
Child support (from a prior marriage)			
Alimony or maintenance costs (from a prior marriage)			
Education expenses			
Private school			
Parochial school			
College			
Religious			
Miscellaneous Pay TV			
Household help			
Entertainment			
Hobbies			
Credit payments Credit card (List all cards with account numbers.)			
Store charges (List all cards with account numbers.)			

	HUSBAND	WIFE	CHILD/REN
Loans (List all loans and identifying information.)			

Note: Make a list of all your expenses for one month or more to ensure that you have not forgotten any expenses—especially major ones.

TOTAL ALL EXPENSES

SUPPLEMENTAL INCOME STATEMENT

This statement should be filled out by anyone who:

1. Operates a business or practices a profession
2. Is a member of a partnership or joint venture
3. Is a shareholder in and is salaried by a closed corporation or similar entity

Nature of business. Check one of the following:

1. Partnership   _____

2. Joint venture   _____

3. Profession   _____

4. Closed corporation   _____

5. Other   _____

Annual income from the business:

1. How often is income received?

2. Gross income per pay period:

3. Net income per pay period:

4. Deductions:

Name of officers of business:

Name of person in charge of financial records:

Attach to this statement a copy of the last three years of your federal income tax returns. Also attach a copy of your most recent profit and loss statement.

Chapter Four

THE MARITAL HOME

One of the most emotional issues in any divorce is the fate of the marital home. Who will stay in the marital home, and who will leave? Couples build their families' lives, often raise children, and live their hopes, dreams, aspirations, and fantasies in the home they have built together.

Determining if you will stay or leave, sell your home and invest part of the proceeds, or stay put can only be answered by working the numbers until you are certain you can afford to stay in the house and continue to pay your other bills. Focus on the business deal.

True, if you have children it is comforting for them to stay in the family house to provide some stability if their parents are splitting. However, if you are not financially ready to do so, deciding to stay can be a devastating mistake. The economic repercussions could drastically reduce your ability to pay for other necessities and hurt your future economic security.

The difficulty is that the marital home often becomes the theater for the divorce war. Neither spouse wants to move out; each desperately wants the other to leave. So when the emotional warfare heightens, every client asks three questions: "Should I leave the house, or should I stay?" "How can I get my spouse out of here?" "If I leave, is it considered abandonment?"

Legally, you are always better staying put. It's worth it to live with emotional discomfort until you get your finances in order. One thing is certain—the cost of separation is just the beginning of the huge expense of maintaining two households. In most cases, this question of whether to stick it out or get out is best answered by weighing all the factors, including the emotional factors, and use a cost benefit analysis to see if the pluses of staying put outweigh the minuses.

The rule of thumb is that it is always less expensive to stick it out in the house as long as you can. That's even considering the cost of professional help to give you the support you need to stay in the house. Treat yourself. Go to the gym or go out with a friend. By saving the cost of another home, you can afford to treat yourself.

One note of caution. You may get different advice from your therapist and your lawyer. Therapists and lawyers often go by different rules. Your therapist might recommend moving out of your house for your emotional welfare. But that might conflict with your financial welfare. You might not have enough money to move to separate quarters. You may need help learning to live in a "divided" home. One man I spoke with told me that his therapist recommended that he move out of the marital home and give away whatever was nec-

> *essary so he could go on living without emotional upset. Ten years later he regretted that he gave up so easily and didn't at least try to stick it out. He lost more financially than he felt necessary and never really made up the loss.*

SHOULD I STAY?

One absolute is that if there is any physical violence, you cannot live under the same roof. You need to get a restraining order and attempt to have your spouse removed from the house. However, *never* lie about physical abuse. If there is a real charge, file for a restraining order. If your life is in danger, do not stay in the house. Seek help at a shelter or with a trusted relative or friend. While staying in a "safe" house, make certain to take the proper legal steps to protect yourself. Consult an attorney or domestic abuse counselor to get the proper advice. Domestic violence can never be ignored or tolerated. If your spouse has any severe psychological disorders, seriously abuses you in emotional ways, or arouses any fears about his or her behavior, consult a professional to help you decide how to protect yourself or your children.

If physical abuse is not an issue, you need to consider other factors. Living in the same house with a person you absolutely cannot tolerate is torture. The one thing you know for sure is that you want this irritant out of your sight! But while divorce proceedings are pending, neither party wants to leave the house, especially if you have children. It is easier to spend time with your children every day when you all live under the same roof. The moment you leave the house, your relationships change. That is not to say that you won't develop new routines, but living in the same house with your children 365 days a year is not the same as seeing them every other weekend or alternating weeks or any other custody arrangement you might construct.

In addition to emotionally changing your relationship with your children, the most important factor and the place where you will notice the biggest change if you move out is your pocketbook. The cost of two households is always more than double the cost of one.

What You Need to Know

Once you are physically out of the house and away from the one place where you and your spouse receive mail and keep records, you will never again have the same access to the financial records you need in order to figure out what your income and expenses are and what assets and liabilities go into the marital pot. Books, records of all your possessions, computers—all will be out of reach. You should never consider leaving before you document, copy, or photograph all the necessary financial records. That said, there are rules you need to know.

Documents You Should Never Leave Home Without!

- *Individual and business tax returns for at least the last three years.*

- *Lists of inventoried items of everything you own. Lists, photographs, videotapes, or any other manner of archiving of personal property items in your home. The more documentation, the better.*

- *All computer records. If you have e-mails stored on the computer, print them. You never know when you may need some information or communication that could be deleted or copied by your spouse.*

- *If your spouse keeps business records on the computer, you need help to get copies. Consult an attorney in your state to get advice*

> *on whether and what records to copy. A lawyer can give you advice on how to obtain copies of records you need without making a formal discovery request.*
>
> - *If you have valuable artwork or antiques and have papers substantiating their worth, make copies. In addition, consult an expert concerning the best way to photograph the artifact or document its existence and valuation should it later magically disappear.*
>
> - *The most recent statements for all retirement plans, bank accounts, and stock accounts.*
>
> - *Copies of all credit cards and account statements.*

The major tasks in the stay-or-go dilemma are to maintain your emotional health and some degree of comfort in an uncomfortable situation. Many couples are all but forced to stay in the house because they cannot afford temporary housing while they are deciding whether to divorce and/or how to split the marital property. If the house becomes a war zone, get the emotional support you need to prepare yourself to live there. This help can come from a good therapist or support group.

The most common complaint I hear is, "I can't pay for a lawyer, so how am I supposed to pay for a therapist, too?" This is often a big problem. My first suggestion is to see whether your health insurance covers visits to psychologists, social workers, or other professionals. If you've never needed professional help before, you may not know whether you have such coverage. If you do, make a list of things you want to discuss with a professional. At the same time, take a look at your financial situation. If you cannot afford separate housing, make certain you tell the therapist that you need help with coping skills to minimize your emotional distress while living in the same house with your spouse.

Or you might seek the services of a professional who uses a sliding scale or charges you based on your income. Groups associated with learning institutions—universities or hospitals—often provide psychological help and will charge you according to how much you earn. Another possibility is to talk through your feelings with a friend or family member you can trust. *Beware:* Be selective and discrete. People getting divorced often "bleed" on everybody, which is not a good idea. First, if you reconcile with your spouse, you will have poisoned others' feelings toward you and your spouse. Second, it is not constructive to spend all your time moaning and complaining. You have a lot of work to do if you are serious about getting a fair split of your assets. It is fine to spend some time venting, but limit that time and confine your complaints to a select few. Third, remember that the things you tell others could get back to your spouse. Hatred won't inspire your spouse to be as generous as possible with your settlement. You may feel better after you vent, but that relief is only momentary. You must always remember that you are in the middle of the most important business deal of your life. Keep focused on numbers and not feelings.

SHOULD I LEAVE?

What if your life starts resembling *The War of the Roses* and you feel you cannot bear another moment in your home? Before making a decision with potentially great economic consequences, consider three things:

Timing: Is this the right time to go?

Records: Do you have all the legal, financial, and business documents you'll need to pursue a divorce settlement?

Information: Do you know the laws that could determine the wisdom or folly of leaving right now?

1. *If you remain married for ten years or longer, you will be eligible to collect Social Security benefits based on your spouse's earnings. This is important if your spouse earns more money than you do. When you become eligible to retire, the amount of money you can collect can be based on your spouse's earnings rather than your own. The Social Security Administration determines how much you can collect by calculating how much your ex-spouse is eligible to collect and cutting that figure in half. This amount is not limited to the amount of money your spouse earned during your marriage; it will also include the amount your spouse earned before you married and after you are separated and divorced.*

   Note: *You do not reduce your ex-spouse's benefits if you do take half the amount. Your spouse will still get the full benefit at retirement age, so this is a win-win situation. If, however, you are the larger wage earner, your Social Security benefits can be based on your earnings. So be careful. If you have been supporting your spouse while he or she is building a fantastic business or getting a degree and his or her future earning potential is big, don't leave a few months before the ten-year anniversary. It may be uncomfortable to stay with someone you can't stand, but it is financially unwise to leave if you are close to your ten-year anniversary. Consider the suffering of staying a wise investment. You have spent many years so far with this person. A little more time could be worth a lot more money. Check with the Social Security Administration for any changes and exceptions to this rule.*

2. *The court may consider your current standard of living when determining spousal support or child support. Let's say you decide to move out of your house and into a small apartment or other inex-*

pensive housing situation. Your spouse could argue that the court should consider only your current, much lower standard of living when it determines the amount of your support. If there is any chance that you will do harm to your case, you should consider putting up with a little discomfort to make certain you do not jeopardize your economic security.

Consider, too, that if you are forced to live in a very small space and do not have room for your kids to stay over, they, most likely, will not feel very comfortable staying with you and you will sacrifice opportunities to spend time with them.

One recommendation I give to my clients is to try to carve out different areas in your home. If you have more than one floor in your house, try to have one spouse stay on one floor and the other stay on another floor. With joint living areas such as the kitchen, you might try to stagger the times you and your spouse use these spaces. Where children are involved, some couples may choose to continue having family dinners; however, with scheduling today, many families cannot manage to all eat at one time. If that is the case, carving out separate times to use common facilities might be easier.

If you are at all doubtful about your economic situation, do your homework about the cost of moving out. Should you move to a house? A furnished apartment? An unfurnished apartment? It may be easier to make just one move rather than a move to temporary quarters and then to a more permanent location. Again, planning is essential! If you do your homework and figure out your costs, you will be able to come to an educated decision about what you can and cannot live with.

3. Is your spouse expecting a large bonus or commission? In some states, the date of separation can have an impact on whether or not you are entitled to receive a portion of the money received. For example, if your spouse is a salesperson and is expecting to receive a large bonus or commission in the near future, it may be foolish to

leave before the money comes in. Similarly, if your spouse is a corporate officer and is expecting to receive stock options, you may want to consider staying if options are property subject to distribution in your state. Also, if your spouse has a short wait before a pension vests, you may want to hang on a little longer before you split.

You must know the facts. Splitting property is a business deal. That is why it is important that you have all the business facts before you make any decisions. In some states, any marital property acquired after separation may not be part of the marital estate. It may be wise for you to consult a lawyer to determine what the laws are in your state regarding property distribution and the date of separation. Again, the least you must do is gather as many facts as you possibly can before you make any decisions about leaving.

4. *You are better able to keep track of what is going on financially if you're still living in the house where the bills and other statements are coming. Once you leave, you lose easy access to this information.*

5. *Find out if your state requires you to be physically separated for a period of time before you can obtain a divorce. If there is a separation requirement, make certain that all your homework is done before you move.*

6. *If you are living separately but under the same roof, do not sleep with your spouse. It may affect when the meter starts running to determine the period for separation—not to mention your emotional state! In some states, if you live separately under the same roof but have sexual relations, even after a few years, this could be considered a "reconciliation" and may interrupt any waiting period necessary for obtaining a divorce. Let's say you are claiming that you were separated and during that time you acquired property you can legitimately claim you received after separation and, therefore, is not subject to property distribution. But then you*

sleep with your spouse. Your lack of judgment could prove to be very expensive, and you may end up dividing property you thought belonged only to you!

One of my professors in law school, trying to explain cost-benefit analysis theory, asked his students the following question: "Just how many nights of your life are you willing to give up to sleep with Raquel Welch?" Cost-benefit analysis is important in measuring your actions while contemplating or going through the divorce process. Every step along the way, ask yourself, "How much will this action or these words cost me, and what am I willing to give up for them?" Make certain that an honest answer is one you can live with.

CAN I AFFORD TO KEEP THE HOUSE?

Remember this: You can never keep the house if you cannot afford the upkeep. The income and expense form you filled out for the last chapter should provide you with the numbers you need to determine the true monthly cost of maintaining your home. The mortgage payment is only the first step toward the upkeep of your house. Add in all the utility bills, maintenance bills, insurance costs, taxes, and repair bills. Don't forget catastrophic costs and emergency repair—the new roof that needs to be put on whenever you can least afford to pay!

Add in all the insurance premiums you need to pay to protect your home if it is destroyed. You can't afford the house if you cannot pay the costs of your other basic living expenses: food, clothing, medical costs, and other basic necessaries. Remember the big picture of all your other life expenses when you are trying to determine what housing you can afford. Your house is not your only expense. Too often people look back after they face financial ruin and lament, "If only I had sold the house I would have had enough money to live." In a good business deal the numbers tell the story.

WHAT ARE YOUR OPTIONS?

The marital home is often the largest or the only asset in the marital estate. Whether or not you can afford to keep the house depends on what other assets are available to split.

If there are more assets to divide, you may be able to trade another asset in exchange for the house. If the house is the only asset, you may have no choice. Before you make any decision, however, you need to get the house appraised. You need to know its true worth. (See valuation in Chapter Five.) The number and diversity of assets in the marital estate may also help you determine what to do. For example, if you own the home with a large mortgage and the only other assets are your retirement accounts, you will have to decide whether it is worth taking money out of those retirement accounts to buy out your spouse's share of the house. Also consider how much you earn, whether or not you have an earning capacity, your age, and other factors. What you most need to be aware of is that there are many economic variables that go into this decision. Consult experts for advice. But before you do, *you* are the one who needs to collect all the information.

If you plan to keep the house, make certain that you will not be house-poor and that you'll have enough cash to pay bills, allow for catastrophes, and still have money for retirement. You are the one who will be responsible for how you will live in the future. The only way not to be frightened by this responsibility is to take charge and educate yourself about what this future involves.

Consider this scenario: In addition to your house, you have a retirement plan in your name. You and your spouse own a duplex that you rent out. Your spouse also has a retirement plan. You both earn approximately the same amount of money. If you are able to pay for the expenses of the home on your salary, you might consider giving the rental property to your spouse, with each of you keeping your retirement plans and you getting the house.

You should fully consider how much your house is worth and how much equity you have in it before you make any decisions. If both of you wish to keep your retirement plans, they will need to be valued. You need to figure out how much the rental property is worth. If you kept the duplex, you would be collecting rent—but you'd also be spending money on the upkeep. You need to also consider an unknown factor: What will your house be worth in the future if you decide to sell it?

In the midst of this complexity and guesswork, ultimately you must decide just how much the house is worth to you and whether any trade-offs are attractive. Again, you do not need to make these decisions on your own. Experts are out there, ready to help you. You just need to get familiar with the concept of the different variables that go into splitting property.

Let's say you have no other assets to trade off and that after working the numbers you decide you are financially able to keep the house. Now you'll need to borrow the money to buy out your spouse's interest. You may want to refinance your home if you have enough equity. Consider the following scenario:

Laura and Bill, who are now divorcing, paid $80,000 for their house ten years ago. They put down $20,000 and took out a 15-year mortgage for $60,000. They still owe the bank $20,000. The house is now worth $150,000. If they were to sell the house at this point, they would get $130,000 minus the cost of the sale and other expenses. Now let's say Laura wants to buy out her husband's share of the house. Because there is value or equity in the house, Laura could take out a larger mortgage—borrow more money from the bank—and give Bill his share.

Don't forget: To refinance in your name alone, you will need to be able to earn enough money and have a good enough credit rating for a bank to go along. Another possibility is giving your spouse a note that you will pay over a number of years. In essence, your spouse becomes the lender or the mortgagor. You can negotiate how much money you will pay each month and the number of years you will have for the payout. It might be useful to use an amortization schedule to figure out how much this amount will be and how much interest you must pay. Again, you need to work the numbers. If Laura and Bill sold the house in the preceding example, they could split the proceeds. Each could take the amount received and use it to buy another house, or each could invest the money until deciding what housing situation would be best.

Often a spouse will want to keep the house until the children are grown. Again, make certain this is a good financial move. (You will also need an expert to help you figure out any tax consequences involved.)

Or two spouses might agree that the spouse who has custody of the children remain in the home for a certain number of years (say, until the youngest child moves out) and sell it at a later date and split the proceeds. (If you decide to do this, consider buying life insurance on the spouse who will be moving out. That will ensure that you can continue to pay the mortgage if your ex dies before the house is sold. That way you can make any payments to the estate, if necessary.) You should also consider the tax consequences of this option.

One family lawyer from the Midwest laments that she has represented a number of women in their second divorces who were trying to keep the same house they got out of their first divorce settlement. Too often she found that if there was a house in the marital estate worth $250,000 and a pension of equal value, often a judge awarded the house to the wife and the pension to the husband. This attorney pointed out that most people wouldn't think of putting a retirement account in another spouse's name upon remarriage, yet they would take the equivalent sum of money that the house represented and put the deed in joint names.

My advice: If you are going to take a house as your part of a property settlement and you decide to remarry, think long and hard before you add your new spouse's name to the deed. If you do, you may end up sharing the house in a subsequent divorce.

I also see men and women requesting that their spouse put a home or vacation property that they owned prior to marriage or inherited during marriage in joint names. Again, it's emotion getting in the way. Houses are more easily tied up with emotions than retirement accounts. I have heard these words again and again: "If you love me, you will put my name on the deed to the vacation home." Sometimes, if one spouse inherits a home after both spouses already own a marital home that they purchased during the marriage, it seems easier to pressure the other spouse to put their name on the deed to the inherited house. Whether it is the nesting instinct or that houses are emotion-laden objects (whereas stock accounts don't evoke such strong emotions), don't put yourself in the position of losing your house, especially if you were divorced before and received it in the last settlement! You could end up homeless.

An attorney from the Southwest feels that too often clients can't afford to keep houses but want to keep them because they are familiar. They become fixated on the nest rather than considering the advantages of selling the house, buying cheaper accommodations, and investing the rest of the money. He recommends using a financial planner who can teach you the best way to manage your financial matters.

THE SHARK ATTACK

When living together becomes intolerable, at some point one party will throw in the towel and move out. Generally, it is best to figure out what the terms of this move will be. Face the big questions: Who will pay the mortgage or rent? Who will pay the other expenses, including utilities and other monthly payments? Who will be responsible to pay for repairs if necessary? It is best to have all these questions answered before one party moves out.

The other major question is this: Who will keep the personal possessions?

Tom and Jill couldn't stand living together any longer. Jill decided to move out. She told Tom she needed some time to save for a security deposit on her new apartment. In December, Tom was positive that Jill would move out in March. He didn't relish the idea of spending the holidays in the house with Jill. It was pure hell coming home and sleeping in the basement. He couldn't wait for her to leave. Although he couldn't stand the situation, Tom was absolutely certain that morally Jill would never consider taking anything with her from the house. Because his salary was double what Jill earned, Tom had made all the major purchases for the house during the marriage. Jill basically paid for groceries and her vacations.

Right before New Year's Eve, Tom arrived home from work to discover that the house had been totally cleaned out. He was enraged. He never believed Jill would do this to him. He didn't take any advice about protecting what was in the house. He hadn't gone to court to file an injunction or a "special relief" to make sure no marital property was removed from the house until the equitable distribution stage of the divorce, when the property distribution would be addressed.

Caution: If your state allows you to request that no property be removed from the house until equitable distribution, you need to consider whether to protect all the property in the house, including valuable jewelry, artwork, and everyday living items. In some states, including certain community property states, the statute or law provides that you may not dispose of property or take property out of the home. In other states, you must file a petition in court to protect your property. If you choose not to do so and one spouse removes property from the home, you run the risk of not getting some or all the property back until you reach the equitable distribution stage. And that might be a very long time—so long that you may have had to go out and buy whatever you needed. Ask yourself this question: Am I better off running the risk of having my spouse come in with a moving van while I am out of the house and taking everything? Or am I better off, even if I anger my spouse, filing a petition to make certain that only those items mutually agreed upon be removed from the house?

Other shark attacks abound. Beware of the spouse who withdraws all the money from your joint account. Because many joint bank accounts are "either/or" accounts, either spouse whose name appears on the account can withdraw all the funds without the other spouse's signature or consent. Lawyers have differing views on whether they would advise their clients to withdraw money. A lawyer from Texas says that the best thing is not to clean out the accounts. "If anything, it will exacerbate the relationship. Take out one-half if you need it. Tell your spouse you've done this and that you will send monthly statements." A lawyer from New England feels it is not a good idea to clean out accounts because judges view this behavior with disdain and have broad discretion to fashion court orders to penalize spouses who take the money. You need to remember that this judge may decide your property distribution and may hold this against you.

The marital home is often the symbol of security and your hopes and dreams. You cannot let this emotion rule any decision you make about your home and your possessions in the house. Do your homework, crunch the numbers, and logically decide what is best for you now and in the future before you make any decisions you will have to live with for a long time.

Chapter Five

EXPERT ADVICE

While going through the divorce process, the last thing you want to hear is that you should spend more money on "experts" to help you navigate your financial future. But sometimes the right advice is worth the money. The challenge is to get the advice that is right for your situation without spending a fortune.

Whether it is an attorney, an accountant, or any other adviser or expert you're hiring, here are a few rules of thumb. Always ask for references. No expert should refuse to give you the names of a few clients whom you may speak with to ask questions. You may want to ask others who have lived through a divorce what experts they used and whether they were satisfied with the results. It is always best to ask those individuals whose case is most similar to your own. However, never rely solely on one other person's referral.

Many of the experts you could potentially work with belong to professional organizations—for example, for lawyers, The American Academy of Matrimonial Lawyers or the American Bar Association—that may be able to refer you to bar associations in your area or give you the names of lawyers in your area who concentrate in family law. (See the sections on each expert for names of organizations.) Always hire someone with whom you feel comfortable. Never let any expert bully or intimidate you.

Other than a lawyer who can give you legal advice, there are various professionals who can help you determine the content and value of your marital estate. Experts can also help you with financial planning.

ACCOUNTANTS

Accountants are trained to look at numbers to determine their "real" meaning. The following is a list of services an accountant can provide:

- *If you have used an accountant in the past and you do not have your tax returns for the past three to five years, you may request copies of back tax returns from the accountant.*

- *If you think your spouse is hiding money, an accountant can review all the relevant tax returns to determine your spouse's true income.*

- *If your spouse owns a business, an accountant can help with an appraisal of the business.*

- *Accountants can show you the benefits and drawbacks to filing joint or separate tax returns after you have separated. For example, if you suspect your spouse has been playing around with numbers and has filed incorrect tax returns, but you have filed jointly (meaning that your name is also on the return), you need to check with your accountant. You could find yourself paying more for back taxes. Depending on the circumstances, you could find yourself criminally liable.*

- *Accountants can tell you the tax consequences of any and all transactions. If you and/or your spouse sell an asset, whether it is a house or stocks, you may be liable to pay capital gains taxes that could eat into your profit. Or suppose you and your spouse are contemplating making an early withdrawal from a pension account. There may be penalties involved. An accountant can work the numbers for you and determine the after-tax amount of an asset.*

- *Accountants can detail for you the benefits of tax credits, deductions, and exemptions, and advise you about negotiating your property settlement.*

Depending on your needs, you may want to consult with any of a number of different kinds of accountants, with different levels of expertise. (See the following box.)

Knowing Your Accountants

Enrolled Agents

A CPA is a certified public accountant. CPAs are qualified to help you with basic tax questions. Make sure you investigate the experience of any CPA you're considering. For tax preparers, look for ATPs (Accredited Tax Preparers) and ATAs (Accredited Tax Advisers). Let's say you are concerned that your spouse may have mishandled your joint tax returns. EAs, or enrolled agents, are tax specialists with the proper credentials to practice before the IRS. Or let's say you have filed joint returns in the past and now you are concerned that you may be responsible for repaying outstanding debts. EAs can come in handy. Forensic accountants are trained to analyze tax returns and other financial information to detect whether or not your spouse may be hiding money.

You should question any expert you hire. Interview at least two or three experts to determine which one you may want to use. You can do an initial interview over the telephone, but ultimately you should meet face to face with any person you're thinking of hiring. Ask concrete questions about accreditation, experience, and expertise.

Your attorney may recommend an accountant and may suggest to you how an accountant can help in your case. If you have a large marital estate, you will want to have someone explain the potential tax consequences in terms that you can understand. Keep in mind that you may have to pay taxes on any sale of property. So when deciding which asset to sell, figure in the amount of possible taxes into your calculations.

For example, if the sale of your home would generate a gain of more than $250,000 per spouse, an accountant can tell you what you can expect to pay in taxes. (The first $250,000 for each individual is generally exempt from taxes. Always check to determine the present tax law.) If you or your spouse will be dividing a pension or retirement plan, you need to know what penalties you will incur if you withdraw money from such plans before you reach a certain age. A good accountant may be able to help you with some financial planning questions, too. If you provide detailed lists of your income and expenses, an accountant may help with a budget and other day-to-day advice.

CPAs are trained to look at numbers and tell you whether books and records conform to the generally accepted accounting standards. But what if transactions are taking place that don't appear on the books? Then you may need to hire special accountants who are trained to read between the lines. Let's say one of the marital assets is a business and one spouse may be hiding assets in the business. You may want to use a forensic accountant or an accountant who knows how to look beyond the numbers to determine the real value.

Does your spouse have a business or hobby for which he or she gets paid in cash? The transactions won't appear in the books. Does your spouse's tax return say he or she earns only $50,000 a year—despite owning a house, a vacation home, two new cars, and a hefty retirement account? It is a pretty good assumption that not all the money supporting these activities shows on the individual return. Some spouses who own businesses put relatives on the payroll who do not really work in the business. After the divorce, the money "paid" to these family members may suddenly reappear in the spouse's bank account! You need a professional who can help you find the money or refer you to someone who can help. The forensic accountant will look at balance sheets and income statements to determine if there are any misstated items or possible phantom income.

How Much Will It Cost?

Accountants, like all professionals, charge different rates. Some may charge hourly, and some might charge a flat fee. Tax preparers generally charge by the hour. A preparer who works for a national chain charges in the vicinity of $150 per hour. You might pay up to $500 an hour for a CPA who will prepare taxes and gives you financial advice during the year. Ask around. Who does your attorney recommend? Who have your trusted friends used, and how much have they paid for the services? Remember, though, that the least expensive is not always the best, nor is the most expensive. Interview, ask questions, then decide.

FINANCIAL PLANNERS

A financial planner can help you look at your budget, income, and expenses and work out a financial strategy. He or she can help you figure out your goals and what you need to save for.

Before seeing your financial planner, have all your financial information on hand so you can show the planner what you own and how much it takes to run your day-to-day household. Give this person a sketch of your "life goals" or plans. For example, if you are thirty years of age and have two children you want to send to college, tell the planner how much money you earn, what you and your spouse have agreed (if possible) to spend for the education of the children, how long you plan on working, and what your goals for retirement are. This may seem overwhelming when you are having trouble getting out of bed in the morning and trying to deal with the world. It is important, though, to map out a game plan, or at least start with a wish list. You might even find that working with numbers or concretes may help focus you.

A planner can help you look at all the assets in the marital estate and figure out which to sell and which to keep. Planners can work along with attorneys to advise you about tax issues. A good planner should be able to give you tax advice just as an accountant might do, but he or she should also be able to help with investment advice.

Financial planners should not give legal advice. Be wary of someone who claims to be an expert in all areas. Some may purport to know everything, even the law. If you find an expert crossing into unknown territory, you may want to consider going elsewhere. Good specialists know their areas of expertise and don't overstep their bounds.

Levels of Expertise

Few regulations govern planners, so almost anyone can use the title. You'll find that credentials and experience vary widely. A CFP is a Certified Financial Planner who earned a degree from the College for Financial Planning in Denver, Colorado. The letters signify that the person has taken certain required courses and passed a test. A ChFC or Chartered Financial Consultant has earned a degree from the American College in Bryn Mawr, Pennsylvania. You're going to have to do your own homework. Word of mouth from trusted friends can be a good start.

There is also the Financial Planning Association (www.fpanet.org; 1-800-647-6340) in Atlanta, Georgia, in which advisers with a CFP, ChFC, or CPA degree can take a day-long examination after three years of financial planning experience and become a member of the Registry of Financial Planning Practitioners (IAFP Registry). You know a person with any of these letters next to his or her name took certain basic required courses and has a working knowledge of the area. (As one very wise stockbroker who was studying to become a financial planner told me, "Even if a person took a lot of courses, if they are arrogant and won't answer your questions satisfactorily, walk away from them.")

How Much Do Planners Charge?

Some planners are fee-only advisers. This means that they do not sell any products and are not making commissions on what they advise you to invest. They are selling you their expertise to devise a plan for you. They may charge a flat fee or an hourly fee. The second type of planner invests your assets, manages your investments, and charges you a fee based on a certain percentage of assets under management. For example, if you have a $50,000 estate, the planner may charge you an annual 1 percent fee or $500 per year. The range generally is between 0.5 and 2 percent annually, depending on the size of your estate. Some may charge more. Beware if the percentage is too high.

It is always best to get a personal reference, but you may want to search the web to get an idea about what different planners charge. Many planners have websites and list their hourly rates as well as the percentage they charge.

Other planners charge a commission on the products they sell. For example, if they sell you stocks or annuities, they may charge you a commission on the sale. If a person is selling a product and will make money, they have a great incentive to sell you that product. That does not necessarily mean that their advice is not good. But it certainly suggests that they may have a bias to give you the advice to buy what they are selling. It also raises issues of ethics or a conflict of interest. You need to ask: Does a person selling a product and earning money by doing so have your interests at heart, or is he or she concerned with his or her own pocketbook?

Some planners use a mixture of the two structures. They will charge both a commission and a fee for services. It is very important that you determine from the outset what you are paying for.

How Do I Select a Planner?

As with all other experts, you need to interview more than one. Just as you will learn with attorneys, it is very important that you hire someone with whose personality and temperament you feel comfortable. There has to be a meeting of the minds.

Getting the best results for you must be the goal. You need to feel you can ask whatever questions and express whatever fears you may have. Just as with attorneys and any other experts, however, you cannot use your financial adviser as a therapist. You need to do your homework, listen to the advice you get, and decide what is best.

Questions to Ask a Planner

- *What degrees do you have?*

- *What professions were you in before becoming a planner?*

- *Do you belong to any professional groups or organizations?*

- *How long have you been a planner?*

- *Do you routinely take continuing education courses?*

- *How large are the portfolios you generally work with?*

- *Do you sell financial products?*

- *What are your fees?*

- *Is any part of your fee based on the sale of a product or a commission?*

- *What percentage of your practice is planning strategies for clients going through a divorce?*

- *Do you send retainer letters explaining what the goals of the engagement will be and explaining what your compensation will be based on?*

- *When you manage an investment portfolio, do you tend to invest in high-, moderate-, or low-risk investments? (In the planner's answering this question, you should be able to discuss your investment strategy with him or her. Discuss your comfort level with taking risks with your money. Would you rather trade a higher rate of return for the peace of mind that comes with safer investments in which you will not lose your original investment or the principal?)*

- *Can you provide references?*

- *If you refer me to another specialist, will you get a referral fee?*

- *Can I terminate our relationship at any time, and is there a penalty for doing so?*

- *What type of follow-up can I expect if I hire you? Do you send reports? Will you make phone calls at intervals? How often can I call you?*

- *Is there anyone else who will be working with you or for you?*

- *Typically, how old are your clients?*

- *When I call you, how soon can I expect a call back?*

- *Here is a brief outline of my finances. Can you give me an overall strategy of how you would invest my money and/or help me pay off my debts?*

A good financial planner will ask to see all paperwork regarding income, expenses, assets, and appraisals. He or she will review the documentation and ask you questions about your goals before giving you advice. Beware of someone who promises you the world and claims he or she will save you from all your debt without presenting you with a clear, concise, written plan. Never allow someone to pressure you into instant decisions. Resist all bullying. Insist on taking time to think, and get other advice if necessary. That applies to any expert you hire.

STOCKBROKERS

A stockbroker is someone who buys and sells stocks and other securities. The best brokerage houses now provide full-service brokers who make trades, manage portfolios, and provide financial planning. Brokers traditionally have earned their money through commissions. In such a setup, the broker is making money on the product he or she sells. However, many brokers now charge differently for their services. They base their fees on the dollar amount they are managing. This lessens conflicts of interest that arise when a broker receives a commission on each transaction. For instance, one brokerage house has a fee-based account with a $50,000 minimum. The fee is 2.25 percent a year for the first $100,000 in stocks and 1 percent for mutual funds, bonds, variable annuities, and cash. The advantage to this system is that it makes the broker's interest and the investor's interest the same. The broker benefits most when the investor makes money.

In a sense, playing the market is akin to educated, legalized gambling. When you choose a broker to manage your money, your hope is that he or she will make a sound, educated guess based on the advice of analysts hired by their firm to pick stocks to buy. Because brokers are salespeople who depend on the research of others, you are placing bets that the house's analysts will choose right.

You should never, under any circumstances, give up all control of your money to a stockbroker—or to anyone, for that matter. You should use a stockbroker for advice. You should, however, do some of your own investigating and portfolio management. By monitoring your investments and the companies you invest in, you have a better chance of protecting your assets.

You must investigate perspective brokers' backgrounds just as you investigate those of all other experts.

Questions to Ask a Stockbroker

- *How long have you been a broker?*

- *For whom have you worked? What professions were you in before you became a broker?*

- *Do you have to make a certain amount of sales a month?*

- *Do you get paid a commission each time I buy and sell a stock?*

- *Are there any charges associated with opening or closing an account?*

- *Do you earn a fee based on the size of my portfolio?*

- *What degrees do you hold?*

- *What is your educational background?*

- *What professional organizations do you belong to?*

- *Can you give me three references?*

- *Do you do any independent research in addition to using your company's research analysts?*

- *In what companies is your firm most heavily invested?*

Two further necessities in your dealings with a stockbroker:

1. *Request a copy of your broker's disciplinary and employment records. You can get this from NASD Regulation, Inc. This is a unit of the National Association of Securities Dealers, Inc. (NASD) (1-800-289-9999 or online at www.nasdr.com). If you look under*

"Disclosure Events," you can check out your broker's disciplinary history. In addition, all brokers must pass a Series 7 test. If you want to make certain that your broker is licensed in your state, check with the NASD.

2. You should receive confirmation statements listing all your transactions. Make certain to read your confirmation statements and verify that they do not contain any transactions you did not authorize. Never allow a broker to convince you that he or she will watch your account for you and that there is no need for you to check your statements.

Let's say you and your spouse have worked with one particular broker and have a joint brokerage account. When you and your spouse separate, or when problems (financial and otherwise) start cropping up, you will have work to do.

1. If there's a possibility your spouse will buy and sell securities without your approval, contact your broker and inform the broker that you want your account frozen. Or tell the broker that no transaction can happen without the approval of both spouses. Confirm these changes in writing. If you have any doubts about your spouse, it is probably better to just freeze the account. You may want to request that your broker place this directive on the online account so any associate who might deal with the account will instantly see it.

2. Make certain you receive copies of your account statements. Too often one spouse moves out of the house and requests that the brokerage statements be sent only to the new location. One lawyer from the West says she deals with brokers all the time who, more used to conducting business with the husband, refuse to send statements to the wife. She has called the brokers' supervisors to report this behavior.

3. *Sometimes a brokerage account will also give checking account privileges. If you have this type of brokerage account, you may want to freeze the account. If you need the money to pay bills, you may want to consider splitting the account in half, setting up individual accounts, and dividing up responsibility for the bills. You could also consider earmarking the account only for large bills such as the mortgage and prohibiting any other checks from being written. You can be as creative as you like as long as you make certain you protect your assets.*

BUSINESS VALUATORS

It's often the case that one member (but not the other) of a marriage owns a business. It may be a small, one-person operation or a much larger enterprise. On many occasions, divorce clients have said to me that they don't want to "take" the business away from their spouses. The idea is not to take anything away, but to realize that the business is part of the marital estate—unless it is excluded by law or agreement as separate property—and you deserve to be compensated with some other asset to equal the value of your spouse's in the business.

The issue then becomes the value of your spouse's interest in the business. That depends on the type of business, the percentage your spouse owns, and other variables. The business will have to be appraised. You will need to hire an expert to determine not just the value of the business but also what your spouse's share is worth.

The first thing you should do is speak with an attorney about the business. It's often the case that the nonbusiness spouse can't find any documents concerning the business at home. If you do know where any documents are kept, make copies of any documents to which you have access. If you and your spouse's attorneys agree to get a business valuation, the valuator should be able to review the books and records of the business and other relevant information.

If you and your spouse own a business together, it should be easier to get documentation. As a partner, you should have ready access to the books and records. If you have all the financial information, supply copies of the records to your attorney and the business valuator. That should include copies of the business's tax returns for the last three to five years. You should also copy any loan documentation, shareholders' or partnership agreements, or buy/sell agreements.

You're finding out the value of the property for purposes of division and for support purposes. If your spouse uses revenue from the business to pay personal expenses, you may need to determine what part of that money should be added back, as it actually counts as *income* to the owner, to give a fairer basis for an award of support. In addition to determining the value of the business, a business valuator can help identify the "income stream," or how much money or income the business actually throws off. A forensic accountant could also assist you in determining such information.

Why Hire a Business Valuator?

If you hire a lawyer, you may wonder why he or she cannot do the business valuation for you. Why do you need to hire another person and pay more money? The answer is that not all family lawyers have a business, financial, or tax background. At a family law seminar on business valuation, it was determined (after an informal poll) that most of the lawyers had been liberal arts majors in college. Law schools do not necessarily require you to take business courses. In addition, because family law involves emotional issues such as custody, lawyers sometimes choose to take specialized psychology courses to better understand the psychological side of divorce. Some schools have specialized J.D./Ph.D. programs. The fact is, your lawyer may be trained in many areas, but complex business and taxation may not be among them. Lawyers should know what tax returns and business papers they will need to obtain and should know how to read and understand these documents. But interpreting the numbers to come up with a specific valuation is not something all family lawyers routinely do. Just as it is wise to hire a lawyer who is completely familiar with family law, you should also allow an expert to give you advice on specialized matters such as a business valuation.

Valuing a business is different from valuing your car or other personal property because a business is dynamic, and many variables can affect its value. Some businesses are also much more complex than others.

Your attorney will want to work closely with the business valuator. Certain legal issues will come into play in the valuation. The business valuator will need to know whether the business should be valued at the date of separation or the date of the hearing or both, which may be a matter of law. Other legal factors may similarly make a difference. For instance, if you are valuing a business for the purpose of equitable distribution, you may want to value the business on a different date than when you are valuing a business for alimony or support purposes. For support, you may need to get a present valuation so you will be able to determine the actual stream of income of the business. Through analytical and investigative procedures, a valuator may also help your attorney figure out what assets are out there and whether they are part of the marital estate.

In some cases, you may not need a valuation. For instance, if the business has recently been put up for sale and you have a firm sale price, you may want to use that number for valuation. Check with your lawyer. If your spouse sold the business in anticipation of the divorce and accepted less than market price, your lawyer may need to get another valuation to get you a fairer settlement. If the business is a medical practice, accounting practice, law practice, or other service business, check the laws in your state to see how such businesses are valued and if they are part of the marital property. Seek your lawyer's advice on the need for a valuation.

How Do I Find a Good Valuator?

You need to get someone who is independent of the business. Your spouse may claim that the accountant who does the books for the business can do the valuation. However, especially if you are the nontitled spouse (the spouse who does not own the business), you will want to get someone who is independent and objective. You need a pair of eyes outside the business to determine whether the purported numbers are accurate or whether there are discrepancies that need to be looked into. You may be able to use the business's accountant to get information, but the information should be evaluated by someone else.

Look for someone who has the proper educational background in finance, accounting, taxation, and, of course, business appraisal. You will also need someone who has experience working in the industry. This experience is especially important if you go to court and your valuator's credentials are put into question. In that case, you will want a valuator who has testified in court. Holding up on the witness stand in a rigorous cross-examination can be difficult. Your attorney should help you ask the proper questions about the valuator's background if you meet with the valuator without your attorney present.

Beware: If you meet with a valuator without your attorney present, your conversation is not protected by attorney/client privilege, and the valuator can be questioned about your conversation in court. To maintain the benefit of attorney/client privilege, your lawyer will need to form the relationship with the valuator. He or she will "hire" the valuator, but you will be responsible for paying the fees.

The rapid growth of divorce has spurred a cottage industry in business valuations. Unfortunately, this also means that business valuation is rapidly becoming a profitable industry. Make certain, therefore, that you check the credentials of any valuator; be sure he or she is qualified as well as ethical. And you must also feel comfortable with any valuator you hire.

Cost of a Business Appraisal

The cost of the appraisal really depends on two things: the complexity of the business and the degree of cooperation between your lawyers and your spouse's lawyers. The more complex the business, the more time it will take. If the valuator has to go through minimal market data to compare one business to others, the process may be much less than if public data and securities information need to be obtained. If the lawyers involved cooperate with one another and exchange relevant documents in the discovery phase of your case, you will not have to go to court to get the information.

Generally, appraisers work on an hourly basis, so the cost depends on the number of hours spent reviewing the material. An oral report will cost you less than a written report. Court time will also add to the expense. If everyone cooperates and the valuator gives a fair oral analysis that both parties can live with, the valuation may not cost too much and the information received may be money well spent.

Expect the valuator to send you a retainer letter detailing the costs and what work he or she expects to do. If you have any questions, call the valuator and get clarification.

To get a list of accredited appraisers in your area, try calling the American Society of Appraisers in Herndon, Virginia. Their toll-free number is 1-800-272-8258. Their website is www.appraisers.

org. You can also get a list of appraisers in your area from the National Association of Certified Valuation Analysts in Salt Lake City, Utah. Their website is www.nacva.com. Their toll-free number is 1-800-677-2009. For more detailed information, see Chapter Seven on how businesses are valued.

CONSUMER CREDIT COUNSELORS

One judge from the Southwest says that the most common problem in divorce disputes is cash flow. One person who can often help couples who seem to have acquired more debt during their marriage than assets is a consumer credit counselor. This expert can help you review your monthly budget, provide advice on the use of your credit cards, and answer general credit questions. If you and your spouse have borrowed a great deal of money through loans or credit cards and have built up too much debt, a counselor should be able to assist in consolidating your debts and advising you how to pay down your bills each month. A counselor can intervene on your behalf and call your creditors to make arrangements for payment plans to pay your bills. Because they negotiate directly with the businesses and other entities to whom you are in debt, their efforts can take a great deal of financial pressure off you. Instead of trying to juggle your bills, you will have a definite amount to pay each month, and the counselor can negotiate who will receive the money. By setting up a payment schedule, you can focus on work, family, and moving on rather than obsessing about your debt.

If you or your spouse have reached a point where you can't pay off your bills and live in two separate households, a counselor can advise you on the pros and cons of declaring bankruptcy. If this becomes your only viable option, you will need to decide whether you and your spouse should file bankruptcy prior to divorce. If a credit counselor advises you to declare bankruptcy, you may want to take that advice to a lawyer to double-check and take steps to protect yourself. Nonprofit organizations either offer counseling free of charge or sometimes for a small fee.

If you need to obtain a copy of your credit report, you can mail or fax a request to a credit reporting agency. You will need to send two pieces of identification along with your request, and within a few weeks you will receive a copy of your credit report. If you have any questions, you can call Equifax (1-800-997-2493; www.equifax.com), TransUnion (1-800-888-4213; www.transunion.com), or Experian (1-888-397-3742; www.experian.com). Under some circumstances, you may qualify to receive a copy of your report free of charge.

REAL ESTATE AGENTS AND APPRAISERS

Often the marital home is one of the largest, if not the largest, asset in the marital estate. If you need to sell your home, you may want to call a few real estate agents and have them look at the property. It often pays to call a local agent familiar with the homes in your area. Get estimates of what similar homes in the area have sold for in the past six months. This will give you an idea of how much your house is worth.

If you need to get a more formal appraisal of your home, you may want to contact a certified appraiser. If you believe your home is worth significantly more than your spouse claims, you may need to use an appraiser who not only is qualified to write a good report using the best comparisons to other homes in the neighborhood and showing why your home is worth more, but who will also stand up under cross-examination by your spouse's attorney. Seek your lawyer's advice as to the best way to find a qualified appraiser.

If you decide to sell your home, you may need to make some cosmetic repairs such as painting or fixing the little things you never got around to doing. Try to get your spouse to split the cost. It may pay to spend a little on repairs to get more for your home and have more to split in the property distribution.

ACTUARIES

If a pension is one of the assets in the marital estate, you may need to have the pension valued. You may need to hire an actuary, a person trained to figure out how much a pension is worth. (Although CPAs and other experts *can* value pensions, an actuary may be more appropriate, depending on the type of pension and its complexity.) Again, your lawyer will be able to advise you.

Actuaries have expertise in interpreting pension plans and calculating their worth. An actuary may work for an insurance company or an employee benefit firm. With the growth of divorce and the corresponding need to determine the value of pensions, the number of actuaries has grown significantly. These experts often become known by lecturing in continuing legal education courses and writing articles for lawyers on divorce. Ask your attorney how he or she knows the evaluator or actuary. Because it may be necessary for the actuary to testify if your divorce goes to trial, inquire whether your lawyer has used the person in the past. Has the actuary testified in other trials? If so, was he or she effective? What were the results?

Tests are given by the Society of Actuaries. Find out if the actuary is an F.S.A., or a Fellow of the Society of Actuaries, or an A.S.A., or Associate of the Society of Actuaries. The Joint Board for the Enrollment of Actuaries gives an E.A., or Enrolled Actuary, designation to actuaries who pass certain tests. There are numerous websites to consult (www.soa.org; www.actuary.org).

Talk to your attorney to figure out which professional to use. It will depend on what type of pension plan is at issue. The various types of plans will be explained in Chapter Six on pensions.

There are a lot of decisions to be made during the divorce process. Your need for expert help will depend on the complexity of your divorce. If you have many assets and the marital estate is large, you may need to use more professionals than if you own no property and are faced with a lot of bills. The best way to start is to gather all the information on your income, expenses, assets, and debts. Take all the information to a lawyer and get advice on what professionals you may need. By educating yourself about the experts you will ask your lawyer better questions, and that, in turn, will help you determine how best to spend your money in learning what your assets are worth and how best to divide them in a divorce settlement.

Chapter Six

PENSIONS AND RETIREMENT

Next to the marital home, a pension is often the next largest asset at issue in a divorce settlement. Sometimes it is the largest. So you need to be familiar with the following:

- *The different types of pensions*

- *The rules and regulations regarding withdrawal and distribution of pension funds (may differ from type to type)*

- *How pensions are valued in divorce settlements*

- *How to decide whether it's worth it to trade a pension for some other asset in the marital estate (or whether to split the pension itself in the divorce settlement)*

Many people contemplating divorce must also consider what they will need for retirement. Much depends on how long you have been married and how old you are. If you are young and able to accumulate funds, you may be less inclined to want to take a portion of your spouse's retirement. If you are older and have been married for a long time, you may need to take a portion of your spouse's retirement as part of your property split if this option is available to you.

There are many different types of pension plans. Many of these plans qualify for special tax status under a federal law called ERISA or the Employee Retirement Income Security Act. This law defines a pension plan as a plan maintained by an employer that provides retirement income to employees. If the plan qualifies under ERISA, for tax purposes, the federal government allows you to deduct any contributions to the plan from your income. The contributions are not taxable to an employee until they are withdrawn. (If your divorce involves an ERISA-qualified plan, you should get a Qualified Domestic Relations Order [QDRO] drawn up if you intend to split the pensions under the plan. See information on QDROs later in this chapter.) These terms are pretty standard, and you might hear your spouse or your lawyer use them.

The two main types of plans are defined contribution plans and defined benefit plans.

DEFINED CONTRIBUTION PLANS

In this type of retirement plan, a certain sum of money is put aside for the benefit of each employee. Every employee has his or her own account. This account consists of the employer's contributions as well as any money the employee may have contributed and earnings from the employee's investment in the plan. It is a given that an employee will receive a certain sum of money upon retirement. However, the exact amount is unknown and may increase or decrease depending on the value of the investments.

There are different types of employer-sponsored defined contribution plans. You may hear other names used.

Kinds of Defined Contribution Plans

- *Profit-sharing plan*

- *Money purchase plan*

- *Tax-sheltered annuity*

- *Stock bonus plans*

- *Thrift plan*

- *401(k) plans*

- *Employee stock ownership plan (ESOP)*

In defined contribution plans, each employee has an individual account balance. Sometimes this means that a certain individualized amount of money is maintained in a separate account for each employee. But there are other ways of doing it. Some employers maintain a larger general pool of money. Then, daily, monthly, quarterly, or at other regular intervals, the pool is valued. Each employee can receive a statement that tells how much the employee's share is worth.

Some defined contribution plans are investment plans that allow employees to make their own investment choices—such choices are generally carefully limited. (This is important to note if you receive part of a defined contribution plan as part of your settlement. Owning such a plan, you may want to continue making your own investment choices. Have this proviso noted in your Qualified Domestic Relations Order if you can continue to make your own investment choices once the account is in your name.)

Consult your attorney to determine if you will suffer any tax consequences should you receive part of a pension in equitable distribution. Depending on the type of plan, if you receive any portion of it as equitable distribution, it is generally easy to segregate the money in the account balance and move it or roll it over to an IRA (individual retirement account) or another similar type plan. When the money is rolled over to another account rather than distributed, you will not have to pay income taxes on the rollover. For your purposes, the difference between a distribution and a rollover is that in a distribution, you would receive the money and be able to spend it or dispose of it as you wish. In a rollover, the money is put into another account, and you are not able to spend it or have access to it at that point in time.

DEFINED BENEFIT PLANS

In a defined benefit plan, the employer promises to pay the employee a fixed or certain benefit when the employee reaches retirement age. Employers make contributions annually to the plan based on sophisticated calculations of how long an employee is likely to live, the length of service, how much the employee is being paid, and other factors.

In defined benefit plans, employers do not deposit money into an account specifically earmarked for an employee. The money goes into one fund, and payments are made out of that specific fund. This type of benefit is not as easy to value as a defined contribution plan.

Contributions to defined benefit plans are generally calculated on the basis of statistics and probabilities compiled by company actuaries. To make certain that enough money will be on hand in the future to fund the pension, employers will deposit the proper amount of money recommended by these experts so retiring employees will receive the exact promised benefits when they retire.

In defined benefit plans, the amount an employee ultimately receives is generally based on a formula. For example, a company may base the benefit on a percentage of the employee's average annual wage over the last ten years of employment, along with certain other factors. A sum of money is determined that then will be paid to the employee monthly starting at retirement.

There are also different ways in which an employee can choose to receive these benefits. A person participating in a defined benefit plan may choose to receive retirement payments for as long as he or she lives. An employee can choose to receive what are known as "joint and survivor annuities."

If you choose a joint and survivor annuity, you and your designated beneficiary both receive benefits after you retire. The added benefit in a joint and survivor designation is that if the retired employee dies, the living spouse will still get benefits. Consider this:

Spouse A and Spouse B marry. A and B divorce. A retires and receives his portion of retirement benefits. B also receives the portion of retirement benefits received as part of equitable distribution. A dies. B will continue to receive benefits until death. B's benefits will survive A's death.

What's the downside? Because the retirement benefits are split between two people, the amount paid to each is less than if just one person was to receive the benefits. Both people will receive benefits until death.

In addition, participants in certain qualified defined benefit plans can choose a qualified preretirement survivor annuity. This means you can choose to have an employer pay benefits to your beneficiary if you die before retiring.

Example: A buys a joint survivor annuity with a qualified prere-tirement survivor annuity provision. A and B are married. A and B di-vorce. A designates B as the beneficiary of the policy. If A dies before his or her scheduled retirement, B can still collect benefits as long as A properly designated B as the beneficiary. Again, under these cir-cumstances the amount of money received will be a lesser sum with this preretirement survivor benefit. However, it ensures that the sur-viving spouse will be assured of a certain sum of money until death.

If you are the dependent spouse and want the added protection of money coming in when you retire, check out your spouse's retire-ment benefits carefully.

Basically, you need to:

- *Know what type of plan you have the option of choosing and how that choice will affect the benefits you may receive.*

- *Ensure that all necessary forms are properly completed by either you or your lawyer so you will not lose any benefits.*

- *Make certain that all beneficiary designation forms are correctly stated and written.*

DIVIDING OR DISTRIBUTING BENEFIT PLANS IN A DIVORCE SETTLEMENT

There are three ways you can split these plans when you split up property:

1. Immediate offset. *If the pension is not the only asset in the marital estate, you may determine the value of all the assets in the estate and then give the spouse not receiving the pension enough money from the other assets to equal or offset the value of the pension.*

2. Deferred distribution. *Suppose you do not have enough money from other assets to offset the pension, or that for other reasons you decide to wait until later to divide the pension. Waiting to distribute the pension is called deferred distribution. In such cases, you will need a Qualified Domestic Relations Order (QDRO) or another similar court document to secure your part of the pension. Make certain that you or your lawyer has properly secured your rights to the pension and any other benefits you may be entitled to receive.*

3. Reserved jurisdiction. *Sometimes this method is used if it is not possible to determine the true worth of a pension. If there are certain variables or unknowns that make it difficult to value the pension, you may ask the court to wait until a later date to rule on how to split the pension. If, for example, there's a chance that your ex will receive a much greater sum of money—say, for example, he or she expects certain bonuses or stock options—and you want to be able to benefit from those unknowns, you may be willing to wait and have a court or other fact-finder (for example, a mediator or arbitrator) determine how much you will receive at a later date. Again, make certain you have taken all the legal steps to protect your right to receive the benefits at a later date.*

The benefit of taking an immediate share of a pension—if this is possible in your case—is that there is a definite end to the matter and you do not have to revisit the issue and deal with your spouse concerning finances once the divorce is over.

Valuing Retirement Plans

Defined benefit plans and defined contribution plans are not valued in the same way. To determine the value of a defined benefit plan you will probably need to use the services of an expert— either an actuary or an accountant with training and experience in valuing pensions. You may need to rely on your lawyer's or adviser's judgment in choosing an evaluator. Because many variables go into determining the worth of a defined benefit pension, there is more likelihood that different experts could come up with different valuations.

Defined contribution plans are easier to value. In many of the plans you can get an account balance on request, meaning you may not need to use an expert to value the plan.

Remember: *Defined contribution plans can take different forms.*

One familiar example is the 401(k) plan. If you are getting a divorce, this type of plan can be immediately split or immediately offset.

If you or your spouse are employed by a tax-exempt organization or by a public school system, you may have a 403(b) plan. These plans may be referred to as tax-sheltered annuities and may be available for immediate offset.

Money purchase plans are profit-sharing plans. They are often referred to as Keogh plans.

Whatever plans you have, you, your attorney, or another expert should examine the requirements and should be able to obtain valuation information. The employer should cooperate and provide you with a description or summary of the plan. If the summary does not contain enough information, obtain a copy of the full plan.

Look at statements of any of your or your spouse's pension plans to see whether any of the names or terminology on page 101 appears anywhere. Again, the more familiar you are with your spouse's assets, the easier it is to find all the information you need.

News Flash

***Certain options available to an employee with a defined contribution plan may affect the value of the plan. Certain plans provide that an employee can make withdrawals in the event of hardship, take out loans, or possibly purchase life insurance. Whoever values the plan will need to know if any of these options were used by the owner and if money was withdrawn from the account.

Certain hybrid plans are part defined benefit plan and part defined contribution plan. These may include any of the following:

- *Cash balance plans*

- *Pension equity plans*

- *Life-cycle pension plans and retirement bonus plans*

- *Floor-offset pension plans*

- *Target benefit plans*

Certain high-level managers in corporations are eligible for other types of employment plans. There are also military pension plans, which are subject to strict governmental regulations.

THE QUALIFIED DOMESTIC RELATIONS ORDER

The Qualified Domestic Relations Order (QDRO) is the written document ordering a part of an employee's pension to be transferred to the nonparticipant or nonemployed spouse. (The nonparticipant spouse is also referred to as the "alternate payee." Other alternate payees can be a former spouse, current spouse, child, or some other dependent of a participant.)

Certain information must be present in every QDRO. It must contain the following:

1. The name and last known address of the participant of the plan.

2. The name and mailing address of any alternate payee included in the QDRO.

3. The amount or percentage of benefits to be paid to each alternate payee, or the method in which such amount or percentage is to be determined.

4. The list or name of each plan to which the QDRO applies.

Every QDRO must list the person(s) or asset(s) to whom the court order applies or the parties involved, for example, you and your (ex)spouse, the particular plan in question, and the precise benefits the parties will receive.

Ask your attorney if he or she writes their own QDROs or whether they use another expert to write the order and ensure that it is put into effect. Make certain that someone who understands the law will be following through and ensuring that all the enforcement provisions have been met. The following are the steps to take to make sure you will get the pension benefit that is coming to you.

The QDRO

1. *Every QDRO must correctly represent what you and your spouse have agreed to in your marital or property settlement agreement. Once you and all the relevant lawyers or experts have drafted and reviewed the order, the QDRO must be submitted to the plan administrator for approval. (The administrator is the person in charge of implementing the plan. If you are not aware if your company has a retirement benefits department, try calling human resources to determine the proper person to contact.) This can take time. Some administrators review the QDROs themselves; however, sometimes outside counsel is used. So the time for review varies. (This can be important if you are named as a joint survivor or have preretirement rights that you could lose if your spouse was to die before the plan is approved. You must be a named beneficiary of an approved plan before you receive your share. You may want to question your lawyer about this. You may want to have your lawyer draft an Interim QDRO or one that will spell out your rights until the permanent order is approved.) Once everyone has reviewed the QDRO, it might be submitted to the court for approval. Different states vary as to whether a judge must sign the order before or after approval by the plan.*

2. *After the QDRO is reviewed, it must be approved and signed by all parties involved. Once the approval has taken place, both the employee and the alternate payee must make certain to notify the institution and/or person administering the plan of any change in address.*

3. *The type of payment method you have chosen—immediate offset, deferred distribution, etc.—will determine when you receive the money. Furthermore, depending on the method, you may or may not suffer tax consequences. Again, that is where the experts can help you.*

There are other retirement plans that do not require a written QDRO but can be split by a court order or other legal document. The plans that fall under this category are Simple IRAs; traditional IRAs; Roth IRAs; SEP-IRAs, or simplified employee pension IRAs; SAR-SEP, or salary reduction employee pension IRAs; and deferred annuities. Your adviser should be able to get the details of each plan and help you determine the value.

HOW MUCH OF THE PENSION ARE YOU ENTITLED TO?

You may hear the term *marital coverture* used for the marital fraction or marital portion. Another term you might hear in connection with the formula is *time rule*. This is an elementary formula.

If you have been married for 20 years but your spouse has worked for a company for 25 years, starting 5 years before your marriage, you are not entitled to a share of his entire pension.

Generally, only the part of the employee's pension earned during the marriage is considered subject to property division as part of the marital estate. To determine the amount of a pension you're entitled to receive, take the total number of years your spouse participated in the pension plan while he or she was married and divide that number by the total number of years the employee participated in the plan.

$$\text{MARITAL PORTION} = \frac{\text{Years participated in pension during the marriage}}{\text{Total number of years participating in pension at date of divorce}}$$

In this example, you would use the number 20 in the numerator, or top of the fraction, and 25 years in the denominator, or bottom of the fraction, to find out the nonparticipant spouse's marital portion of the pension.

As with all mathematical formulas in divorce, other variables might go into the valuing of a pension. If the situation is too complex to permit use of this simple formula, you may need a CPA or an actuary to give you a pension valuation. These experts will consider variables including different rates of interest. An employee may also have a choice of retirement dates, any of which may alter the valuation. If an employee chooses to retire early, he or she may get a smaller pension than if they retired later.

Some plans provide for cost-of-living increases that may need to be added in and valued. You also need to determine what happens if you wait or defer the distribution of the pension until the employee spouse retires. Will the nonparticipant spouse benefit from the appreciation of the pension during the years the couple were not married?

The only certainty with divorce valuation issues is that they can be complicated. Creative lawyers and valuators come up with different angles every day. At the very least, you will need to discuss the type of plan with your attorney or adviser to determine the minimum valuation you should expect.

HOW A GOOD EXPERT CAN HELP YOU GET WHAT YOU NEED IN A QDRO

Suppose you are a parent, and your ex is supposed to make child support payments. Suppose he or she is unemployed or just refuses to pay child support to you. Let's also assume he or she has a large sum of money in the form of a pension plan. You could provide in a QDRO for a plan administrator to make arrangements for payments to be made to the child as an alternate payee if the employee/participant fails to make the proper child support payments. However, you will need to check to see whether this option is available to you in your state.

Similarly, if an employee or plan participant has to make periodic alimony payments and a pension plan exists, you may be able to structure the payments as pension distributions by utilizing a QDRO and naming the former spouse as alternate payee. Knowing that the payment will come from an independent or third party rather than your ex may give you some added assurance that you will receive the money. (Other ways to secure alimony payments will be discussed in Chapter Fourteen on property settlement agreements.)

If you are concerned that your soon-to-be ex is contemplating bankruptcy, you may want to consider having a QDRO drafted that makes provision for you to be an alternate payee of a pension plan your spouse may have. You may be able to prevent your spouse from avoiding an obligation via bankruptcy by setting yourself (rather than your ex-spouse) up as a payee from a pension plan. Again, you need to consider the circumstances and check the law in your state.

WHAT HAPPENS TO PENSION BENEFITS IF AN EX REMARRIES?

Sometime after your divorce your ex-spouse remarries. A few months later he or she dies. You expect to receive part of his pension benefits. However, his or her new spouse could step up to claim those benefits if your QDRO has not been carefully drafted.

Federal tax law regarding qualified pension plans provides certain automatic survivor benefits. Under these laws, the participant's current spouse at the time the participant retires or, if the participant dies before he or she retires, at the date of his death, is considered the participant's "surviving spouse." This means it is presumed that a current spouse is the alternate payee or is the person entitled to the remaining pension benefits upon the participant's death. For a former spouse to ensure that he or she will get the benefits they expected or contracted to get, there must be a provision in the QDRO stating that the former spouse will remain the "surviving spouse" for all preretirement and retirement benefits, whether or not a death or remarriage occurs. Nightmares like these are another reason drafting the QDRO is important. If you are to be a surviving spouse, you need to make certain that the expert has made the proper provision in the QDRO to protect your rights. Again, this is where money to an expert who knows the law will be money well spent!

If your ex-spouse's pension has a cost-of-living clause that provides for certain increases based on a raise in the cost of living, your lawyer may be able to include a clause in the QDRO so you could benefit from any additional increases that your ex may receive. Your lawyer may also want to make some provision should your ex become disabled. If there is a provision in your spouse's retirement benefits that he or she is eligible for disability payments, your lawyer may want to consider securing for you the right to receive a portion of that benefit when your ex starts to receive the payments. Again, you will need a lawyer or expert familiar with pensions to draw up a document that will help you get the benefits to which you are entitled.

Pensions can be very valuable assets. You can't afford not to know whether your spouse has a pension and what that pension is worth. You must make certain that you are correctly named as beneficiary of any proceeds from any pension plan. Timing is critical. If you need to get an interim or temporary order until a final order is written and approved, have your lawyer do so. Check to see what type of pension is at issue and how it is valued. At the very least, you must recognize that a pension is a very valuable asset you can't afford to overlook. Check your state laws to clarify how pensions are treated in your state.

Chapter Seven

VALUING BUSINESSES

Statistics show that more than 22 million people own their own businesses. The 1999 census states that more than 16 million people are self-employed. If we assume half these people who are married will at some point divorce, that leaves a great many who will need to have their businesses valued as part of the marital estate during their lifetime.

If you have built a business while married and are contemplating divorce, you will have to determine what part of your business will be considered marital property. Most people going through a divorce do not want their spouse to take any part of the business. That means you will have to come up with other assets to trade for the value of the business. Possibly you have put money into a pension plan and you can roll over part of the plan to your spouse. If you don't have other assets, you will have to face the fact that you might have to borrow money or possibly sell out of your portion of the business.

Whatever you decide to do, the one thing you will certainly feel is that your business belongs to no one but you! You will not want your spouse to get any of your sweat and blood. You may feel that it's not part of the marital estate! The law, however, will *not* take this position.

Whether you are the owner or partner (titled spouse) or non-owner (nontitled) spouse, the first thing you need to do is to get a copy of the business tax returns. Those documents should tell you what type of business entity the business is and how much the business is earning. (See later in this chapter for the tax forms you will need and what they might be able to tell you or your expert.)

The difficulty in valuing a business at divorce is that there are many ways to value a business. However, unless you write a pre-nuptial agreement with specific provisions on how to deal with your business interest in the event of divorce, you will need to value your business when your marriage ends.

There are difficult issues and questions that need to be faced. Is it a big company with a financial audit each year, or is the business a sole proprietorship that runs its expenses out of the owner's personal account? On what date should you value the business? If you value it at the date of the hearing and you have been separated for three years, should your spouse benefit from the part of the business that grew during your separation? If you value the business at the date of separation, do you also need a valuation at the date of the trial, so you can figure out how much money or income the business generates as a basis for the proper amount of child or spousal support? And how can you protect yourself and ensure that your spouse can't "double dip" and get credit for a percentage of the business in equitable distribution and then also take a part of your earnings or income for support?

Just as with pensions, the different methods of valuing businesses may seem confusing. However, it is important at least to know the basic terms. You will, at the very least, want to meet with a business valuator along with your attorney to see how extensive a valuation you may need. Definitely bring your attorney. You will want him or her to ask the questions, because any communications between your lawyer and the business valuator are privileged. If you go without your attorney, that privilege does not exist. However, you will feel more empowered and part of the process if you go along, understand some basic terms, and follow the conversation between the experts.

Some courts will expect business valuators to use certain methods when valuing a business. These can include the following.

FAIR MARKET VALUE

Fair market value, as defined in Treasury Regulations, is the standard often used for tax purposes—what a willing buyer will pay a willing seller when neither party is under any duress or neither is forced to buy or sell. Both the buyer and the seller must have reasonable knowledge of the facts of the business.

The problem with this standard is that it is based on the value the business would have if there were a cash sale. In a divorce, you are not putting the business up for sale, nor do you have a willing buyer or a willing seller. And the last component in the Treasury Regulations definition—that neither party should be under compulsion to buy or sell—is certainly not the case. One party is, in effect, selling a portion of the business under compulsion in a divorce. And both parties do not generally have the same level of knowledge about the business. Nevertheless, courts sometimes impose this standard of valuation on the parties in a divorce process.

> One way to think about the value of a business is to ask this question: How much money will the business generate in the future? The market price of a business is really someone's opinion of the business's future earning potential. If you are looking for money to help pay bills in the future, you will look for a way to get either a piece of the business or its cash equivalent in the property distribution, or some of the future income as support.

Business valuators will typically look at the accounts receivable and the debts of a business when considering fair market value. Valuators also may look at the sales of other comparable businesses. For example, if you own a hardware store or other retail business, you might consider what other business of a comparable size and location sold for in the past year. (If you are the nontitled spouse and you disagree with a valuator's comparison, you will need to argue that the business really wasn't the same.) If you own a restaurant, you can look to recent sales of restaurants of similar size and type to get an idea of the restaurant's value. In addition, there are books and computer programs that can give you formulas to determine valuation. These formulas are generally expressed as multiples of gross revenues, operating income, and other factors. These rules of thumb are generally taken from comparable or similar business sales.

These and other methods can give you a starting idea of the value of a business. Some valuators will call business brokers to find out what similar businesses have sold for in the past. Another way is to look for tax guidance and what factors the Internal Revenue Service uses to determine the value of a business.

REVENUE RULING 59-60

Courts will often use the IRS analysis or Revenue Ruling 59-60 as a basis for determining the valuation of stock in a closely held company. In the tax arena, this ruling has also been used for valuing other types of business entities. This ruling looks to different factors and requires an analysis of each when valuing a business:

- *What type of business is it?*

- *What is the history of the business since its inception?*

- *What is the general economic business outlook?*

- *What is the business outlook for the specific industry?*

- *What is the financial condition of the business?*

- *What is the book value of the stock?*

- *What is the earning capacity of the company?*

- *What is the dividend paying capacity?*

- *Does the business have goodwill or other intangible value? (See later in this chapter for an explanation of goodwill.)*

- *Are there sales of stock, and what is the size of the block of stock to be valued?*

- *What is the market price of stocks of corporations in the same or a similar business?*

Keep in mind that these factors come from tax rulings as tools used to determine the worth of a business. Valuing a business for tax purposes is different from valuing it for divorce purposes. However, courts grasp onto these guidelines as one method of valuation.

WHAT DOCUMENTS DO I NEED?

There are certain documents your attorney might want to obtain. A business valuator may also visit the business and review books and records. Some of the documents that will be important are the following:

- *Any and all financial statements and tax returns of the business for at least the past five years. A business valuator will want to see the trends of the business. Has business increased or decreased?*

- *Profit or loss statement or income statement. These will disclose the net income and the costs and expenses of the business.*

- *The balance sheet of the business. The balance sheet is a statement of the financial position of a business. It will show the debts and assets.*

- *Lists of stockholders or partners indicating the amount of stock or percentage interest owned in the company. This can tell you whether an owner has a controlling share or a minority interest in the company. An owner who controls decisions may have an interest that is worth more than an owner with no say.*

- *The capital accounts of the partners if the business is a partnership.*

- *Statements of retained earnings. (Retained earnings is profit that is reinvested in the business. Retained earnings may be used for legitimate business expenses; however, sometimes owners can hide money in the business by disguising income as retained earnings. Instead of taking the share of income rightfully due, the owner may keep the money in the business and claim that the money is needed for business purposes.) This should also show up on tax returns.*

- *List of cash accounts and any cash investments.*

- *List of aged accounts receivables (money owed to the business but not yet paid).*

- *List of aged accounts payable (money owed and not yet paid).*

- *Copies of any business plans (budgets and projections).*

- *List of officers' and directors' compensation.*

- *Schedule of key person's life insurance and other insurance—property, casualty, and/or liability.*

- *List of existing contracts.*

You will also want any partnership agreements that may be in effect. If the business is a corporation, you will need the bylaws and the articles of incorporation. If there is a buy/sell agreement or any legal contracts, you may want to copy them.

Keep in mind that your lawyer will be able to request these documents from your spouse's lawyer. The preceding list contains items your lawyer may request for the business valuator. If your spouse keeps business records in the home and you have access to these records, it is always beneficial to obtain copies of any documents you can. This list can help familiarize you with documents you should copy if you have the opportunity.

The following is a list of tax forms. Your experts should be able to review tax forms to determine the proper level of income received from a business from all sources.

Tax forms and other documents you may need, depending on the business:

- *Form 1065 partnership tax return*

- *Form 8825 (Lists rental property.)*

- *Schedule C Form of 1040*

- *Schedule K-1 for partnership returns (You may want to check Line J, Box B to see how much money a partner put into the business during the year. Also, Box D shows what money might have been taken out.)*

- *Form 1120 S (For businesses that are incorporated but make an S Corp election for tax purposes. Check Schedules M-1 and M-2.)*

- *Form 1120 Schedule E (Will tell you the ownership percentages of officers and their compensation.)*

A concept that comes up in valuing businesses and is very important in valuing professional degrees is "goodwill." There are many definitions for goodwill. Goodwill is the increase in earnings or value brought on by return or repeat business. Does a customer return to a business because of its name? For example, will you buy Nike running shoes because you are familiar with the name of the product? If so, Nike's name recognition gives the company added value and, therefore, goodwill.

If, as with the case with Nike, a particular company's reputation gives it an advantage over another company, there is most likely goodwill. This is called "enterprise goodwill"—goodwill associated with the name of a business. In contrast, "professional goodwill" is tied to the reputation of an individual and what that person does for or contributes to the business. For example, you might choose to go to a particular doctor because you like her or him, and you return to the practice because of that one particular person.

If you are divorcing, it may be critically important to you whether the courts in your state consider professional goodwill as part of the marital estate. If you supported your spouse throughout school, or if you sacrificed a career so you could raise children, you may feel that you deserve a piece of your spouse's professional practice when you split property. Only certain states consider goodwill of a professional practice to be part of the marital estate. The states now including professional practices in the marital estate are Arizona, California, Colorado, Connecticut, Indiana, Kentucky, Maryland, Michigan, Montana, Nevada, New Jersey, New Mexico, New York, North Carolina, Ohio, Oregon, Virginia, and Washington. Because family law is an ever-changing field and a good lawyer can make a creative and persuasive argument, in the future, more states may change their rules on this issue.

Some courts, however, reason that professional goodwill is personal to an individual and not capable of being divided as an asset. But even in these states you may still be able to get compensated with spousal or child support. A professional's income is always the basis of a support order. Professional goodwill translates into dollars. These dollars, or the income generated by professional goodwill, can always be considered when determining the basis for a support order. A professional, be it doctor, lawyer, therapist, accountant, dentist, or any other professional, earns a certain level of income each year. The courts won't make a distinction between income from goodwill and ordinary income. Don't despair, then, if the court disagrees with your argument that professional goodwill should be valued into a business that you want divided for equitable distribution purposes. If you are requesting spousal or child support, the income from the business is the basis for the support order. Therefore, if you lose out on getting this portion of money as part of the property division, the money itself is considered as income for support purposes.

Now consider this scenario: A spouse has given up professional opportunities and stayed home to raise the children or be a homemaker. Can he or she claim that his or her contribution to the partnership of the marriage should carry a dollar value? Many family lawyers who view marriage as a partnership continue to argue that a dependent spouse, or the spouse who sacrificed his or her career for the sake of the marriage or the family, should be compensated for the sacrifice. The equitable distribution process is supposed to take into consideration the contributions of each spouse to a marriage. So if one spouse contributed by spending more time with child-rearing while the other spouse could go out and work without having to worry about car pools and other child-related activities, both spouses should be compensated for their work. The law continues to change in this area. Persuasive attorneys will continue to press for the passage of new law.

CELEBRITY GOODWILL

Matrimonial lawyers also are pursuing the concept of "celebrity goodwill." Say you are married to a person who earns a great deal of money in the entertainment industry or in sports. Or say you are married to a businessperson who can earn money because of his or her name and separate from any corporate entity. In such cases, if you divorce, you may be able to argue that the person has celebrity goodwill. For example, Bill Gates, Donald Trump, Cindy Crawford, and Tiger Woods can earn money because they have achieved a certain celebrity status.

If you are married to someone who is well known and earns a great deal of money and you feel you have a right to participate in their good fortune because you helped them and contributed to their success, you may want to check your state laws to see how the courts treat celebrity goodwill.

VALUATION REPORT

Once the evaluator has thoroughly reviewed all relevant documents, he or she can issue a preliminary oral report. Sometimes spouses can settle their case based on the verbal findings alone. This is certainly less expensive than having a written report, and certainly less expensive than going to court. If both parties seem able to live with the number the valuator comes up with, this agreement could be enough to settle the property division. However, such an agreement is not always possible. Generally, one side (and sometimes both) will feel that the business is worth either more or less. In that case, the valuator will have to write a written report that states the nature of the business and all the facts and documents relied on to reach the final appraisal. If you and your spouse have chosen one valuator to appraise the business and one of you is unhappy about the appraisal, you will have to decide whether the person unhappy with the report needs to get another valuation. Often, much cost and expense can be wasted on dueling experts. If you think there is a chance you will need a second opinion, you may want to start off with your own evaluator.

Some lawyers feel that each party needs his or her own evaluator. Ask your lawyer for advice on this point. You may feel you need a warrior for your cause. You need to consider how much money is at issue, how big the business is, how much money it brings in a year, whether or not it is a cash business, and how much money you can afford to spend to value the business. Sometimes the expenditure and aggravation aren't worth it.

If you need a written report, that report should give a full description of the business, the method of valuation, the name and qualifications of the evaluator, the names of relevant documents that were reviewed, and a full explanation of the rationale for the evaluation. The report should state the date on which the business was valued. It should also state the reason for the valuation.

Any relevant industry standards that the evaluator may have used should be included as well.

WHEN BOTH SPOUSES ARE IN THE BUSINESS TOGETHER

Difficulties arise when both spouses work in a business together. Some people have divorced and remained successful business partners. That's fine if you can do it. But in many instances of divorce, spouses want to end all aspects of their relationship and not stay together for any reason, which is understandable enough. But if the business has been the principal source of livelihood for the spouses and the family, it may seem unthinkable to kill that livelihood. In such a situation, you may need to figure out which breadwinner is the most valuable for running the business. This may be difficult emotionally, but keep in mind that equitable distribution is a business deal. Look at the bright side: If both spouses work in the business, both will understand the finances of the business. But if both spouses have been using the business for their own personal expenses such as transportation, car insurance, travel, and entertainment, and you decide that only one spouse will remain in the business, you will need to figure out how the spouse who will lose this benefit can be compensated for the losses.

Questions that need to be asked include: How much is the business worth, and should the departing spouse continue to receive a share of the profits? Will he or she receive other compensating assets? If both spouses built the business, how will the departing spouse be compensated? Can the departing spouse find employment elsewhere? Will it take an extended period of time for the departing spouse to get other employment? If so, should that spouse receive some form of support until he or she finds another job?

You do not want to ruin a good business. Figure out how to compensate both spouses for their efforts. You may want to speak with a neutral third party to determine whether both of you can continue in the business together. Some couples with children feel that because they will always be partnering as parents, they won't mind continuing the partnership or business relationship also. Again, just make certain you are emotionally able to do so.

Chapter Eight

STOCK OPTIONS AND OTHER COMPENSATION

Today, many people who work for companies receive, besides their pay, other assets or perks that are much harder to define in terms of marital property. Employers often try to lure people away from other jobs by offering signing bonuses. To induce an employee to work and give his or her all to the company, an employer might give incentive bonuses. And as we witnessed during the dot.com craze in the 1990s, start-up companies may lure workers by offering stock options as part of their benefits package.

When it comes to divorce, these other forms of compensation can be difficult to quantify and value. A regular salary is a defined number you can use to determine how much spousal or child support one person should pay another. When you divide a house or a bank account, you can easily assign a value to these items. It is also easy to determine when these items were purchased. If you accumulate any of these items during the marriage, they are considered the marital assets and are divided when you split up your property.

However, quantifying and valuing other forms of compensation is a complex area that many professionals, including lawyers and judges, do not always understand. You may have to depend on an expert to help you figure out how to value these perks when dividing your marital property. It's a good idea to understand certain basics so you can work along with your lawyer or financial adviser. Understanding the basics may also give you a sense of whether your expert is the right person for you.

As you try to discover perks and other forms of compensation, keep in mind that you're looking for any form of compensation for services rendered while you were a "partner" enabling your spouse to earn these benefits.

The questions "What is part of employment compensation?" and "How should that compensation be valued?" are continually changing and expanding in divorce law. It helps if you think of a marriage as a partnership and the breakup of a marriage as a process that will involve each former partner getting his or her financial contribution out of the partnership. The job for you and your lawyer will be to come up with a proper analysis of your soon-to-be-ex-partner's compensation—all aspects of it, from salary to bonuses to perks—and what part of that compensation should rightfully be yours.

If your contribution to the partnership—your marriage—enabled your spouse to go out and work while you took care of the household, you may want to go after a share of all the benefits along with the salary. Conversely, a breadwinner will want to determine what part of his or her benefits are not part of the marital assets. Good lawyering plays an important role in each of these arguments.

You may ultimately choose to walk away with enough assets to ensure a good lifestyle even though you may decide not to have every asset valued down to the last penny. However, you should knowingly understand what assets belong in the marital estate. If you decide that it is not worth spending thousands of dollars to value stock options or other benefits and you feel that you don't need to fight for the absolute highest possible valuation, you need to at least understand what rights you may be giving up. (Valuing options and other perks can get expensive because you are engaging high-price professionals to do complex work. Discuss with your lawyer the pros and cons of property valuation as it applies to your case.)

Each state has laws that variously determine whether assets in the marital estate should be valued at the time of separation, the date of the filing of a divorce action, or the time of the hearing. The date of valuation can greatly affect the value of the benefits. It's also important to understand the way different courts look at benefits and perks—it determines the way they are divided at divorce, or if they are divided at all. Is a particular benefit a reward or compensation for services performed in the past, or is it payment for services that may be performed in the future? You need to determine according to your state's laws, what services (your own and your spouse's) have been and ought to be compensated and when these services were performed (during the marriage, after separation, or any time up until divorce).

STOCK OPTIONS

Sometimes employees are offered the right to buy stock in their company at a specific price during a specified period of time. This is called a stock option. There are many variables associated with options—variables that often make them difficult to value.

For purposes of divorce, you need to consider the following questions:

- *Is the stock option part of marital property? In most states, if a spouse received the option during the time of marriage, it will be considered part of the marital estate.*

- *How do you value the option? And when? Because there can be wide fluctuation in market value, check with a lawyer to determine when the options will be valued in your state.*

- *What are the tax consequences when the option is exercised?*

In most states, if stock options are granted to an employee while he or she is married, the options will be part of marital property. Courts also recognize that an option may be granted in recognition of past services. If a spouse received an option after the parties separated but the option was supposed to reward an employee for past services that were performed while the couple was still together, the employee's divorcing spouse could argue that the options probably belong to the marital property. So it's important to determine when the services rewarded by the option were performed. If the options are granted when a couple is still together but the options are supposed to be a reward or incentive for services to be performed in the future, you still can argue that the options are part of the marital property, as they were granted while you were still together. You should look for any connection between the stock options and the period you were married. (Of course, if you are the spouse holding the options, you will want to prove that there is no connection between the time the options were granted and your marriage.)

It is important for you to ask your lawyer if he or she knows how stock options are treated in your state. Many lawyers who do not specialize in family law may not be aware of how the courts handle this issue. Getting a lawyer who knows the area is important if you or your spouse works for a company that gives stock options as part of employee compensation or pay. Valuing options is a specialized field. You really need a trained professional to help you with the valuation.

If you live in a state where the property is valued at the date of the hearing rather than on the date you and your spouse separate or the date you file a divorce complaint, your lawyer will need to find out if any stock options were given to an employee at any time up to the hearing. Sometimes a spouse who knows he or she is divorcing will have his or her employer hold off on giving options until he or she is out of the marriage. But getting to court often takes a longer time than you may like or expect. If your state values property at the date of a hearing rather than the date of separation, you may stand to benefit by the delay. One thing you should keep in mind about divorce is that you should use every possible advantage you can legitimately get!

There are different ways to value stock options.

1. *One method used is called the* Time Rule. *Basically, this method attempts to determine when the option or the right to the option is established. Again, this question is whether the option was earned during the marriage, that is, whether the services the option is rewarding were performed while the couple was married. The courts use a formula that determines what portion of the options were granted during the marriage, values them, and compensates the nonemployee spouse accordingly.*

2. *Another method of valuation is called the Black Scholes method. Basically, this method is a very complex calculation concerning itself with the stock's price, the "strike price" or exercise price of the options, the risk-free rate of return equal to the duration of the*

option, the volatility of the stock, the dividend yield, and the dura-
tion of the option. You will need a valuation expert to help you
with this calculation.

Can I Take Part of the Options, or Should I Choose Another Asset?

You may have to decide whether (a) you want to have the stock options appraised and then receive cash or an equivalent asset equal to that amount, or (b) take a part of the stock options themselves. Be aware that some stock options cannot be transferred to someone other than the person to whom the options were given. If you need the money, or if you are the type of person who would rather have the certainty of cash, you may want to have the options valued and then take cash or another asset in their place.

If you have done your income and expense statement and know how much you need to live and how much you need for retirement, you may decide cash in hand is better than the uncertainty of stock options. Granted, you may not get dollar-for-dollar credit for the options, but if you receive compensation with which you are satisfied, you may not want to spend a great deal of money fighting over how much the options are worth.

Another very important consideration is what tax consequences you may suffer if you exercise stock options. Is the money you receive when a stock option is exercised taxed as ordinary income or at capital gains rates?

Your goal is to get the greatest amount of property with the least amount of taxes. Check with your expert or adviser for advice on the best way for you to split your marital property. Get advice from your lawyer or accountant about the latest tax rulings. The tax rulings on these issues are constantly changing and evolving. Find an adviser you trust to help guide you with these decisions.

Are the Options Property to Be Distributed in Equitable Distribution or Income Available for Support Purposes?

Another crucial question is this: Should the court consider stock options and other benefits as (a) property to be distributed in division of property, or (b) part of income to be included in support? The distinction is this: If the stock options are considered property, the options go into the marital estate. If, however, the options are considered as part of a spouse's income, then, when the money is received, the amount will be included as income that is available for support purposes.

Another question to ask a lawyer: If the options are marketable and not subject to restrictions, can a court force your spouse to sell the options, so the money can be included in the income available for support?

This is an area where good lawyering can make a difference. It would be a terrible thing if you were to include the options as part of marital property—and then find the court, at a later date, acting as if that money still exists as income and bases child or spousal support calculations on it. (*Note:* If your spouse receives a part of your pension as part of the property split, make certain that the income you may receive from a pension payment is not included as part of income to determine support calculations.)

There are many different types of options an employee can receive. Here are some of them:

- Incentive stock options. *These are options granted by an employer to an employee to buy stock at some specified time in the future. There are often restrictions on whether such options can be transferred to another person.*

- Phantom stock options. *These options are a promise by the employer to pay money or property to an employee in the future. The promise is unfunded and unsecured.*

- Phantom stock plans. *These are an interest in the equity of a company and allow the employee to participate in the growth of a company, if any.*

- Indexed options. *An employee gets a certain sum of money representing the gain in company stock if the price of that stock exceeds a specific stock index.*

- Stock appreciation rights. *An employer can grant an employee a right to take, either in cash or in stock, the increase in value of shares of stock over a period of time.*

- Restricted stock. *This is stock that has limitations on how and when you sell it.*

Tax Consequences

For tax purposes, you should ask your adviser about nonqualified stock options and incentive stock options. Nonqualified stock options are taxed at the time you exercise them as wages subject to regular income tax. Incentive stock options are not taxed as wages when you exercise the options but rather they are taxed at the Alternative Minimum Tax rates. Ask an adviser about the differences in taxation.

FLEX BENEFIT PLANS

Employees often can choose what benefits they would like to receive based on a certain dollar amount. Sometimes these benefits are taxable, and sometimes they are nontaxable. This type of compensation enables an employee to put money into benefits and avoid or delay paying taxes on that sum. For example, an employee can choose to have an employer pay for insurance premiums, unreimbursed medical expenses, or medical deductibles.

Sometimes an employee can take advantage of subsidized day care a company might provide. Other benefits might include health clubs, meal plans, tickets for sporting events, and life and disability insurance. Any and all of these are benefits a person would have to pay for if the company did not provide it. And in all such cases, you can argue that the dollar value of these benefits should be added into the evaluation of your spouse's compensation. Remember: *Don't* ask for this if the benefit is helping you as well as your spouse. If you and your spouse both reap the benefit of a subsidized child-care facility, for example, you may want to continue enjoying this benefit without endangering it in the divorce settlement. You need to thoroughly think through all your arguments before you finally take your stand on what you want. (It makes sense to negotiate with the other side about which benefits will be off the table.)

You may need a lawyer to help you discover all the compensation your spouse receives. Again, you will always need to factor into any court battle just how much the legal fees and other expert fees will be. It is best to make an educated decision. Have your lawyer and any other relevant advisers help you look through tax returns and other documents to get an idea of how much money could be at issue. Then carefully decide on a course of action.

Chapter Nine

INSURANCE

The last thing you want to do when you are facing a divorce is shell out money for insurance premiums. It may seem the money could be better spent on things for the house, for yourself, or your children. However, do not consider ever going without health insurance, car insurance, property insurance, or disability insurance! The last thing you can afford to face is another crisis. Too often clients have decided they couldn't afford to pay insurance premiums—only to face a disaster a few months or years down the road that they really were unable to handle. Consider this:

Jane and Tom were married for ten years. Both were professionals. At the time of their separation, they had two children who were eight and nine. Jane had custody of the kids, and Tom moved one hundred miles from Jane. Tom saw the kids every other weekend at first. Tom remarried and had another family.

Jane made certain that the children saw their father once a month and spent time with him during holidays and during the summer. Because Jane was used to working and her main concern was keeping custody of the children, she didn't get child support, but she did have Tom pay for the children's health insurance. She maintained her own health insurance through her job. She realized that she always would need to work, and she bought a disability policy in case she ever was injured so she would be assured of an income. After four years, Jane got tired of paying high premiums and she dropped the disability policy.

About six months after she dropped the policy, Jane was shoveling snow and hurt her back. She took sick leave for a month. Her back problem worsened, however, and her doctor told her that she would be unable to sit eight hours a day. Because her job required that she sit at a desk all day, she had to quit work. Jane was able to get unemployment for a while.

Jane, however, was faced with having to file for child support. Tom told her that if he had to pay child support, he would file for custody of the kids. Jane was frightened and was really angry with herself because she had dropped the disability policy. It was hard enough trying to pay for her own medical insurance, not to mention the mortgage on her house. She considered not paying for her health insurance, but she knew that if she were disabled further she would face losing the kids. Jane realized that she would also have to get some training and try to find a new job.

Ultimately, Jane sold her home and moved in with her parents, who lived in the same school district where her children attended school. She was able to maintain custody and get part-time work while she built her own consulting practice. She realized that without her parents to help her, she would not have been able to maintain custody and build a new life. Jane regretted not paying for the disability premiums that would have allowed her to maintain her independence.

Just as you never approach marriage with divorce in mind, you never really want to think about all the other things that can happen to you in life when you are in the process of divorce. However, during divorce is when you most need to be realistic and take the necessary steps to protect yourself and your children. No one likes paying insurance premiums, but if some disaster occurs, you need to know you won't be forced to give up your home or forgo proper health care or other necessities—not to mention a custody battle a nasty ex might threaten if you file for an increase in child support.

Following is a list of types of insurance that, ideally, you should always maintain:

- *Health insurance*

- *Disability insurance*

- *Life insurance*

- *Homeowner's insurance*

- *Car insurance*

- *Property insurance*

- *Long-term care*

HEALTH INSURANCE

Health insurance is a must in modern life. But divorce can complicate the health-insurance picture. Especially during this stressful period, you do not want to allow your medical insurance to lapse. Clients often have told me that they didn't want to get a divorce because they had certain health problems, they were covered under their spouse's health insurance, and they were frightened that they would not be able to pay for their own health coverage.

Whether you claim that the insurance premiums, as part of your expenses, should be paid by your spouse as spousal support, or whether you pay the premiums yourself, you need to know what your rights are concerning the coverage itself.

If your spouse is the person in your family who maintains health coverage through work, you are entitled (if your spouse works in an office that employs twenty people or more) to obtain coverage through COBRA or the Consolidated Omnibus Reform Act. This federal law provides that you can get coverage for up to thirty-six months after your divorce through your spouse's existing policy. You will be required to pay the premiums; however, this will allow you to keep your health insurance while you investigate other policies. You can call the benefit supervisor at your spouse's employer and get whatever information you may need. If you intend to work, you may be able to get medical coverage through a new job.

If your spouse works in an office that employs fewer than twenty people, you will need to find out if you can obtain insurance through your spouse's plan. Most states provide that companies with fewer than twenty employees can get some type of coverage through the spouse's existing plan. If all else fails, call your insurance agent, Blue Cross, or another medical provider to see what your options are.

If you find out how much the insurance will cost, you should include that figure on your expense form. You will need this knowledge not only for your own peace of mind and planning, but also because if you know the amount of the insurance, you can request that your spouse pay for all or part of the premium if you do not earn any money or if your earning capacity is not great.

Covering the Children

If you have children, you will need to ensure that your spouse will continue to pay for their medical coverage. Federal law requires that a child cannot be denied coverage if one parent has medical coverage through work. (The rationale for this law is that children will be taken care of as long as a parent works and has the benefit of health insurance through the job.) It is, however, always wise to put a clause in any agreement that covers child support that the parent with the health coverage will continue to provide medical insurance for the children.

Note: Some people believe—wrongly—that you do not need to pay for a child's medical insurance if that child does not live with you. Nor does taking the child as a dependent on the tax return have any bearing on whether you must pay for health coverage.

It may not be convenient to use your spouse's health coverage if he or she lives in a different state. It can get awkward. But if that is the coverage available to you, take advantage of it.

Sometimes, both parents will continue to cover children on two different health policies. It may, however, be a hassle to deal with the health insurance companies' questions about who is the primary insurer. (*Note:* Discuss with your spouse who will be the primary insurer if this affects your children's coverage in any way.) There may be conflicts, duplications, confusions. It may be aggravating to straighten out which company will pay. However, you are much better off dealing with such problems than not having any coverage at all.

If you have any doubts about whether your spouse will continue the health coverage for your children and you are their custodian, you can get a Qualified Medical Child Support Order or QMCSO. This is a court order that directs the noncustodial parent with health insurance to have the children covered under the policy. A QMCSO can also stipulate that the parent with custody of the children will be reimbursed through the insured spouse's insurance. I always have

> clients who are not holders of insurance complaining that they paid
> for certain medical services and their ex-spouse refused to reimburse
> them, even though that spouse could recover those expenses through
> his or her insurance.

DISABILITY INSURANCE

No one wants to think about suffering a disabling illness or accident. When you are going through a divorce, the last thing you
want to consider is the next disaster! Yet this is the very time that
contingency planning is critical. Most people rely on their spouses
to help them if they are unable to work and earn a living, so in the
event of a divorce, disability insurance is extremely important. If
you have children, you will need to consider how you will support
yourself and your family if you suddenly became disabled and unable to work.

If you work, you may get a certain amount of sick leave. You
may also be able to continue health coverage through your work
for a certain time if you become disabled. But if your medical condition renders you permanently unable to work, you will need
other income and other sources of insurance. You may qualify for
Social Security Disability. However, if you earn a good salary,
your expenses are high, and you want to continue living a certain
lifestyle, you will need to find out how much disability insurance
will cost.

Speak with a financial adviser to determine what size policy
you will need to support yourself and any dependents. If you are
the primary breadwinner in your family and have dependent children, you may be reluctant to shell out for disability insurance.
Now is not the time, however, to forgo premiums on your dis-

ability insurance. At a time when you may feel that all everyone wants you to do is pay bills, it may be tempting to cut your expenses and not pay for disability insurance. But saving money this way is penny-wise and pound-foolish. You will feel even worse if you let your disability insurance lapse and something happens to you later. (*Note:* If you collect disability and you pay child and/or spousal support, you should make certain provisions in your child and/or spousal support agreement for a cut in your payments commensurate with your insurance proceeds. See Chapter Fourteen on property settlement agreements.)

LIFE INSURANCE

If you have children and are receiving support, or if you have any obligations under a property settlement agreement that stipulate you must pay money in the future, make certain that you have enough life insurance to secure the obligation.

Tim and Debby, now divorced, were married for thirteen years. They have two children, twelve and ten. Debby works part-time, and Tim is employed as an engineer. Debby will be the primary custodian of the children. Tim has agreed that, in addition to child support, he will pay Debby a small monthly amount in alimony for four years. Tim and Debby have signed a property settlement agreement as part of their divorce settlement. Tim is paying child and spousal support. However, Debby is concerned that if Tim was to die before he finished making the alimony payments and before the children were out of the house, Debby would not be able to earn enough money to support the children and herself while the children were still at home. Tim agrees to buy a life insurance policy that, in the event of his death, would pay Debby about the same amount of the child and spousal support payments due under the property agreement. In addition, Tim agrees to buy extra insurance with the children named as beneficiaries so they would have enough money to go to college if he was not around to pay.

No one likes to shell out money for life insurance premiums, but it's a necessity, especially if your ex-spouse is making support payments to you or your children. You have expenses, bills to pay, and a life to live. And if you have children, you have to make certain they will be cared for if the person making the payments dies.

Types of Life Insurance

The aim of buying life insurance is to make sure that if your ex-spouse dies, you or your children will receive the payments agreed to in your marital settlement for the time specified. Different types of life insurance policies are available. You can buy either a term-life insurance policy or whole-life insurance policy.

1. *Term-life insurance will pay a specific amount to the person or persons you name as beneficiary. As the name suggests, it remains in effect for a specific period of time. (Some policies allow you to convert the policy to a whole-life policy when the term ends without taking another medical exam. This is valuable if the person whose life is insured becomes ill and is no longer able to get insurance.) Generally, you want your ex-spouse to buy insurance for the length of time that he or she owes you money or has other outstanding monetary obligations. Term-life insurance is less expensive than whole-life insurance.*

2. *Whole-life insurance is part of a class of insurance policies collectively called "cash value insurance." As the name signifies, a whole-life insurance policy stays in effect for a person's entire life.*

   Whole-life insurance has a cash value, and you will need to find out that value when you are listing and valuing all your assets. The cash value of a whole-life policy is a marital asset if the policy was purchased during the marriage or with marital funds.

Some policies can also work like an investment plan and may pay benefits after a certain period of time. You will want to ask your insurance agent or financial adviser to get this information for you if you are not able to figure it out yourself from the policy. Check with an adviser to determine which type of policy is best for your circumstances.

The Cost of Life Insurance

You can get an idea of how much insurance will cost you by going to any number of websites (for example, www.quotesmith.com or www.intelliquote.com). In addition, you can contact insurance companies or an insurance agent to help you with the information. You will need to figure out how much coverage to buy to replace the amount of income or support you'd lose should your supporting spouse die. Also, you need to create an accurate and detailed income and expense statement for yourself to help you determine living expenses to cover with insurance.

Beneficiaries

When purchasing an insurance policy, you will need to determine the beneficiary, or the person who will be receiving the insurance proceeds. This can be a complex issue in the divorce situation. Too often, a person names a beneficiary in a policy and forgets to change the name of that beneficiary when they divorce. The insurance company will then go ahead and give the proceeds to the person named in the policy. If you have a property settlement agreement in which it's determined that your ex-spouse should receive insurance proceeds, or if you have made any other agreement as to how the property should be split, it is important to make certain that the beneficiaries on all your insurance policies are the same as those named in any agreement you might have. Conversely, if you are expecting to be a beneficiary, you should demand proof that all the necessary papers are signed correctly, verifying that you are the beneficiary. Follow through. Make certain that all written documents conform with the insurance policies.

When going through the divorce process, most clients tell me that they are going to remove their spouse's name from their life insurance policies the minute they separate. You cannot always do this. Check with your lawyer or adviser before doing anything precipitously. Too often in divorce actions, people do what makes them feel better emotionally. However, this can end up hurting you legally. A judge may consider the removal a cheap shot and may hold it against you. If you feel you have a legitimate reason, go to court and ask permission to change the beneficiary. Don't act vindictively!

Making Sure Premiums Get Paid

You need to make certain that the person responsible for paying the life insurance premium makes the payment. (This is true for health insurance and any other insurance premiums as well.) You may want to add a clause in the property settlement agreement that the spouse not paying the premiums will receive copies of canceled checks or other proof of payment. You may also want to have the insurance company notify both spouses of payment and of any changes in the policy (for example, cancelation or changes in the coverage, premiums, or provider). Sometimes lawyers provide that the nonpaying spouse shall pay for any missed premiums and the spouse who was required to make the payment will have to reimburse the other spouse as well as pay any costs for enforcing this clause or provision.

Here are some other questions you need to answer:

- *Who owns the policy?*

- *Can the policy be transferred to anyone else?*

- *Can the person who owns the policy take out loans against the value of the policy? If so, can you restrict the amount the person can borrow?*

Tax Consequences

As with all other divorce issues, you will want to check whether there are any tax benefits you can take advantage of when paying the insurance premiums. If you are paying alimony and you pay for life insurance premiums, you can take the premium payments off your taxes as deductions if the person who is receiving the alimony owns the life insurance policy.

HOMEOWNER'S INSURANCE

Make certain that your house and your personal property are insured through homeowner's insurance. Again, you may need to check with an agent or research your policies to check your coverage for your house, condominium, and all personal property inside. There are different types of homeowner's insurance available. You may need to value your personal property to determine the amount of coverage you need. In addition, most policies should cover any liability in case someone falls or is injured in your home. As with all other insurance, you will need to get quotes of how much it will cost you to buy the insurance. You will then need to include the cost of insurance on your expense form.

If you don't own a home but rent, check with your landlord to see what, if any, coverage the landlord has and whether it covers anything besides the structure of the apartment or rental unit. You can buy renter's insurance to cover your personal property inside the rental property. Some policies will also cover you if you are sued should someone get injured while in your apartment. Check to see if the insurance will also cover alternate housing should your apartment become uninhabitable for any reason.

CAR INSURANCE

If you own a car, you need to keep current on your car insurance. If you and your spouse are currently insured on the same policy, find out how much individual coverage will cost you. You can call your insurance company and get a quote for individual insurance. You may also wish to research other companies and policies. It may be that you will want to get all your insurance coverage through one agency and use one insurance agent. Whatever you decide, you should independently find out, either online or by consulting with agents, approximately how much it should cost you for all your insurance needs. Add it all up, and put the number on your expense form.

If you have children who drive, include the cost of their insurance on your expense form. Make sure the person responsible for paying the car insurance has done so. Nothing is worse than putting children in the middle of a nasty divorce. If you have any doubts that your spouse will continue to pay for auto insurance, make certain that your property settlement agreement stipulates that he or she must do so.

UMBRELLA POLICY

Depending on your lifestyle and your needs, you may want to find out how much an umbrella insurance policy will cost. An umbrella policy is additional insurance coverage which will pay benefits to you once all of your other insurance—car, homeowner's, or rental—has reached its limits or, for some reason, does not cover certain incidents. Most insurance policies insure you or your property up to a certain limit. If you own valuable property such as artwork, you may want to make certain that your insurance policy will reimburse you dollar for dollar should that property be lost. Or you may need another policy that can cover any excess cost. (Check the policy. It may provide additional coverage for things not covered by your homeowner's policy and other additional coverage such as excess medical coverage.)

Your insurance needs will depend on the amount and type of property you own. If your possessions are modest, you may need homeowner's or equivalent insurance. If your marital estate is large and you want to make certain that the property you receive can be replaced should disaster strike, you need to discuss your needs with an insurance professional or expert.

LONG-TERM-CARE INSURANCE

Depending on your age, you may want to consider buying long-term-care insurance. This type of insurance covers medical and support services in the event of a long-term illness or incapacity. Some policies cover in-home care; others cover nursing home or other institutional care.

If you have an insurance agent, you may want to inquire about the differing types of policies. Some policies may even convert to annuities after a certain period of time.

Remember this: Once you're divorced, you may no longer rely on anyone but yourself for your financial security. Make certain you have at least considered what would happen if you became incapacitated over a long period of time. Insurance in all its varying forms should not be overlooked in a divorce.

Chapter Ten

THE GOOD LAWYER

Choosing the right lawyer for your case is not easy. Unfortunately, what you ultimately receive in your property settlement and how much you have to pay to get a good settlement will depend not only on who you choose to represent your interests but also on your spouse's choice of lawyer. The first question clients generally ask me is, "How much will it cost me, and how difficult will it be to get divorced?" The answer to these questions depends on how much you will have to fight in court and how much you will be able to negotiate out of court. Too often, that depends on the lawyers involved.

Educating yourself about the possible issues in your case will go a long way in helping you determine whether a lawyer is the right one for you.

Although you are probably full of doubt at this moment in your life, having chosen the wrong mate and now separating, you will have to trust your instincts as well as do some research to find a lawyer who not only knows the law but with whom you can communicate. It is not enough to have a smart lawyer; you also need someone with whom you feel completely comfortable and can be completely honest. You will need to be able to ask questions and have them answered to your satisfaction. You need to understand your case and how your lawyer is going to pursue it. No question is a dumb question.

QUALITIES TO LOOK FOR

Many people may advise you at this moment to get an inexpensive lawyer so you can save money on legal fees and keep as much money as you can for yourself. The problem is that the least-expensive lawyer can sometimes end up costing you more. Someone who doesn't know the law will charge you for the time and effort it takes them to get up to speed. Hiring an attorney with a good reputation in the community may help you settle the case. Your spouse's lawyer may be more inclined to settle than to fight it out in court if your lawyer is known for being a good advocate.

You need an effective and efficient lawyer. Any lawyer can go to court and protract a case by fighting over each and every issue. The only people who generally benefit by such protracted litigation are the lawyers. True, in certain cases it may be necessary to fight over many of the issues. In most divorce matters, however, a "good" lawyer should be able to negotiate many of the issues and fight over only those issues that absolutely cannot be resolved out of court. Most good matrimonial lawyers will know how to keep the battles to a minimum. Especially in custody cases, the last thing you want to do is drag your kids to court. Not to say that you will never set foot in court, but you do need to choose your battles wisely.

THE "GOOD" LAWYER

A good lawyer is one who will work with you to make certain you get all the information necessary to determine what property is in the marital estate. If you prepare for your meetings with your lawyer and gather as much information as you are able, a lawyer won't waste time and money to duplicate material you already have retrieved. A good lawyer may check the accuracy and completeness of your information by sending out interrogatories or making other discovery requests to ascertain that the material is accurate, but the bottom line is that your lawyer is working for you and should be able to work along with you.

You and your lawyer should be able to sort out your respective roles in the divorce settlement. In cases where complex business questions are at issue and stock options or other employee compensation are involved, you may also need to hire an expert or financial adviser, or, depending on your level of expertise, you may be able to help with this. If there is a large estate at issue with numerous assets that need to be valued, with luck and hard work you will get enough in the property division to more than pay for this expert advice.

That said, an experienced lawyer with a law school degree and years of experience should know what battles need to be fought. Too often I have heard people going through a divorce remark that they thought they must have paid too much because their lawyer made the process seem easy. That ease may be a sign of a good lawyer. A good lawyer can make resolution look easy, as well as lessen the agony of an exceedingly painful process.

BASICS FOR DIVORCE LAWYERS

Divorce law is a complex field that encompasses more than just domestic relations law. A good matrimonial lawyer will have a foundation in tax law, property or real estate, business valuations, accounting, pensions and related fields, finance, and a rudimentary knowledge of bankruptcy. If your case involves child custody, your lawyer should have more than a basic working knowledge of psychology. When your case concerns questions of custody and finance, your lawyer absolutely will need to know how to cross-examine an expert witness on any related matter. In addition, every transaction or property transfer will need to be examined, and the tax consequences of each action needs to be taken into consideration. At a minimum, your lawyer will need to direct you to a good accountant or financial consultant who will give you the proper tax advice. The least any family lawyer must do is recognize all the issues involved in your case.

Jan and Bill were married for twenty years. Both worked during the marriage and put money into retirement plans. Bill's pension plan was the larger of the two. They purchased an expensive home in which they raised their three children. Bill received many stock options from his employer. When they went into divorce proceedings, Jan wanted to keep their large home and agreed not to take any part of Bill's stock options or larger pension plan. Shortly after their divorce, Jan decided she didn't need to keep such a large home. After all, her kids were grown and out of the house. After she sold the house, she was shocked to learn she had to pay capital gains tax that ate into the money she intended to use for her retirement. Her attorney had failed to inform her that she would have to pay capital gains tax and that, had she wanted to sell the house, it would have been better to sell it while she and Bill were married. Had they done so, the tax bill would have been less. What Jan considered her nest egg turned out to be quite a bit smaller than she had planned. She was forced to work for a longer period of time than she had wanted.

Your lawyer needs to inform you of all economic consequences but can't do so unless he or she is aware of your thoughts and intentions. When you are considering whether or not to keep the house, a good lawyer should go over all the income and expense statements and help you decide what decision makes best economic sense. As discussed in Chapter Four on the marital home, too often divorcing spouses can become emotionally attached to a house when they lack the money to maintain it. You need to make educated decisions, and a lawyer should be able to help you do so. You may want to discuss these economic issues with your financial adviser, not your attorney. However, your lawyer should make you aware of the need to consider the economics.

It is always better to get a lawyer who concentrates in family law. A family lawyer may charge you more than a lawyer who handles a few divorces a year, but the expertise is generally worth it. That's not to say that every family lawyer is a "good" lawyer, but as a general rule, their expertise and experience count a lot. Your lawyer's job is to fight for your share of the property, but a lawyer without the proper expertise isn't likely to do a good job. The advantage of using a lawyer who concentrates in family law is that such a family lawyer is well versed in the law in general and the crucial specialty. Lawyers who do not practice divorce law on a routine basis do not always keep up with that area. If your lawyer does not realize that your spouse's retirement pension is a part of the marital estate, you can't begin to get your fair share of the property. If your spouse works for a corporation and gets stock options and your state law provides for inclusion in the marital estate, your lawyer needs to not only be aware of this fact but also to work to have them included.

Your lawyer needs to know what questions to ask to get the correct information from you. At the very least, if you know nothing about your family finances, your lawyer will need to send out interrogatories or written questions to your spouse's attorney to make certain that all the property in the marital estate has been discovered.

Susan and Dave called it quits after seven years. Susan interviewed attorneys and decided that because she was a professional she could pay for a big-name lawyer. All Susan got after two months was a $15,000 bill. She discovered that although she used an attorney considered a "player" in the field, the attorney pawned her case off to an associate who spent a great deal of time researching and telephoning opposing counsel. Susan had assumed that she'd get personal attention and that only the big name would be working on her case. In addition, her bill included the time that a paralegal and secretary spent working on the matter. What was worse, Susan found out that the associate and the big-name lawyer went to court without telling her, and she had to pay for both attorneys' time in court as well as travel time to and from court. In addition, Susan discovered afterward, that the lawyers filed the case in the county where her husband lived. They could have filed the divorce action in the county where she lived, where the masters and judges were more sympathetic to working mothers. The lawyers filed in the county more conveniently located to their offices. It saved Susan in travel time, as the attorneys worked right across the street from the courthouse, but it ended up costing her big time in her property split. She didn't know what questions to ask the attorneys in the initial interview. Her experience taught her what questions to ask, and eventually she went to another lawyer.

Questions to Ask Your Lawyer

- *Do you practice family law exclusively? If not, what percentage of your cases are family law cases?*

- *How long have you been practicing family law?*

- *Do you represent mainly men or women? (Most family lawyers will have experience representing both. It is always best to be able to argue effectively for either side.)*

- *Who will be working on my case? Will you be the only lawyer, or will there be associates working on the case? What are your billing rates per hour? What are your associates' rates? Will both of you go to court hearings, and if so, will I have to pay hourly fees for both of you?*

- *Do you have support staff who will be working on the case? What are their hourly rates?*

- *Do you feel you personally have enough time to pay attention to my case, or do you anticipate that the case will be primarily handled by an associate? Will your associate do all the preparation, and will your role be to appear in court?*

- *Will you personally answer and return my phone calls, or will I be speaking mainly with your associate, secretary, or paralegal?*

- *Do you attend continuing legal education classes and seminars? How many hours a year?*

- *Do you work with experts? What are the names of the experts you use? When do you use experts? What are the rates of the experts you use?*

- *Do you try to reach a negotiated settlement, or do you think it is best to always try cases in court?*

- *Will I be able to assist you in my case by doing any work to cut costs?*

- *How much do you charge to make copies of documents, and can I do that for you?*

- *Can I make the necessary telephone calls to get the necessary pension information, tax returns, and bank account statements, or do you require that someone from your office do this work?*

HOW MUCH WILL IT COST?

You will want to get information about costs. As with anyone you hire, you want to avoid hidden charges and other nasty surprises. The following questions may help you figure out how much the lawyer charges and whether the costs differ for different tasks:

- *How do you bill? If you bill hourly and I call you for three minutes, do you round off your bills to the quarter-hour? (Some lawyers will charge for only the three minutes of a three-minute phone call. Others may bill a minimum of a quarter-hour or round off the minutes to the next highest five or ten.)*

- *Do you charge a minimum when drafting a document? Some lawyers will charge a base minimum (say, five hours) to prepare any written agreement no matter the actual time spent. This is the case even though most family lawyers have certain forms on their computers and do not draft each and every word separately for every document. You don't want to be paying for your lawyer to reinvent the* wheel. However, your case will be unique in certain ways, and real work will be required to modify the forms. If you have very few assets and the divorce is fairly clear-cut, it may not take ten hours to draft an agreement. On the other hand, many cases can get quite complex. If a lawyer has to customize your agreement, it can take a great deal of time. Again, depending on the complexity of your case, the drafting of certain portions of your agreement may take a lot of thought on your attorney's part. You want that. You don't want to end up five years after your divorce not being able to enforce a provision in the property settlement agreement because your lawyer neglected to draft the proper clauses to protect you.

- It's a good idea to determine the relative simplicity or complexity of your case at the very outset. If you think your case is simple, question your lawyer in the beginning about the possible issues and their level of complexity. You should understand up front how complicated your case is and how costly your divorce might be. Find out about rates and billing by asking:

- Are your rates the same for the time you spend in court and the time you spend on the telephone?

- Will you send me an itemized bill monthly? Some lawyers send monthly bills; others send bills at different intervals. Find out when you will receive these bills. Some lawyers will tell you orally how much you have spent if you ask. You can also ask your lawyer to give you a ballpark estimate of the time necessary to work on a particular matter. If you want to limit your expense and to a certain amount, discuss this at the outset with the lawyer. Ask: Will you go over that bill with me, or is there a charge if I have a question?

- Will I be responsible for paying all my attorney's fees, or will you be able to get my spouse to cover some fees?

- Do you require a retainer? (A retainer is an advance of legal fees.)

Most lawyers require one. The amount can vary greatly. The more financially sophisticated a case, or the more hotly contested the custody issues, a retainer could be as little as $500 to $1,000 or as high as $25,000. (One judge says the statistic that most surprised him is that the average divorce costs $20,000.) Lawyers generally bill hourly against this retainer. Many lawyers will require you to pay additional retainers once the original is depleted. But some lawyers will request a nonrefundable retainer, which means that they can keep the entire amount even if you do not use the time. Lawyers justify this practice by explaining that they hold open time to handle your case and should be compensated for this. Although this is true, it is always better to be able to get back whatever portion of your retainer is not used. If you decide to switch attorneys, to reconcile with your spouse, or for any other reason do not use all the money you pay for up front, you should be able to get that unused money back. If your lawyer will not agree to this, you will have to decide whether it is in your best interest to stay with the lawyer or move on to someone else.

Hourly Rates

Lawyers' hourly rates vary from state to state and from county to county within each state. Some lawyers may charge $150, while others may charge $500 or more. You will need to decide how much you can afford to pay. That's another reason for asking your lawyer to give an opinion as to whether your case is complex or relatively clear-cut.

Your behavior as a client will have a lot to do with how much you spend on your divorce. Even simple cases can get expensive if you choose to fight over every issue. In addition, you will be charged for every phone call. That's a good argument for using your phone time judiciously. Your lawyer is not a therapist. If you choose to use him or her as a therapist, you will have to pay for the advice. So come to all discussions (whether by telephone or in person) prepared! Gather all your information together. Don't impulsively fire off a call to your lawyer. Write down your questions and concerns beforehand and think about them first. If you call asking questions because you want reassurance constantly, even a simple divorce will get quite costly. It's not the lawyer's job to remind you that the tab is running It is their job to sit and listen and then bill you for their time. Use it efficiently!

Your Costs

You will be paying for more than just lawyer's fees. You also will have to pay all costs and expenses connected with the divorce. You will be responsible for the following:

- *All court costs. It will cost you money to file your divorce complaint. Fees vary. To find out the fees before hiring a lawyer, you can check with the prothonotary's office or the clerk of court in your county. (Check your telephone directory for the courthouse listing or the main telephone number for city government. If all else fails, try directory assistance or the local bar association.) Each additional pleading, each official document, including motions and petitions, requests for special relief, and any additional filings, will cost you money. Your lawyer does not pay for this; you do.*

- *Expert witness fees. You'll be paying the fees of any expert you use, whether it be a forensic accountant, vocational expert, business appraiser, custody evaluator, or any other outside adviser. There are some ways to keep costs down. Your attorney may feel that it is acceptable to use one expert rather than dueling experts and may be able to negotiate with opposing counsel to split the fee. You will still be responsible to pay your part of the bill.*

- *All expenses for duplicating documents, postage and courier fees, telephone calls, and any other costs associated with your case.*

- *Ask your lawyer what costs he or she expects will arise in your case. Make certain to review your bills to ascertain if you are paying for any unexpected or unexplained expenses. Don't be afraid to question your bill. Remember, however, that you are required to pay all legitimate expenses. A good lawyer works hard and deserves to get paid for time spent and all legitimate costs. You need to reach a level of trust with your lawyer so you feel you are both doing what is expected.*

- *Travel costs. If your lawyer needs to travel for any reason, you will be required to pay the cost. If travel is required, speak with your attorney so you have a full understanding of what costs you might incur. It is always better to ask than to be surprised with a bill you didn't expect. If your attorney will need to commute a long distance to court, you might want to ask him or her if it would be better to get local counsel.*

WHERE DO I LOOK FOR A LAWYER?

Over the years, I have asked my clients how they found me. I have received many varied answers. Other clients often gave a referral. Other lawyers (family law and others) gave my name out. So did therapists and doctors, professors, and even staff in the family court system. A referral from a satisfied client is a good way to get the name of a good family lawyer.

Most county bar associations keep lists of names of attorneys who practice family law. After you obtain names, you may want to make initial phone calls to the lawyers' offices to see if you can find out what that attorney's hourly rate is and figure out which one will fit into your budget to initially narrow down the list. Call attorneys you know to get a recommendation. Attorneys who do not practice family law can often make a referral to an attorney who does. If you respect a person's opinion and they think highly of an attorney's competence, you are off to a good start.

You can contact the American Academy of Matrimonial Lawyers in Chicago (www.aaml.org; 312-263-6477). Members of this group must have concentrated their law practice in the field of family law for ten years and have passed a test. If you interview a lawyer who is a member of the Academy and you cannot afford the hourly rate, you may ask that person to recommend a lawyer in the area who does not charge as much but has expertise in the field. Membership in the Academy is an excellent credential, but there are also good attorneys who are not members of the Academy. You may also contact the American Bar Association's Family Law Section (www.abanet.org; 312-988-5613) to get a list of divorce lawyers in your area. Martindale Hubbell is a national directory of lawyers (www.lawyers.com). Lawyers are listed by geographical area and specialties.

If you are seeing a therapist, you may want to ask the therapist for a recommendation. Personal and family counseling, as well as custody, are often issues in divorce cases. That means that psychologists and psychiatrists often work with attorneys who practice family law. Again, if you trust your therapist, it is worth asking for a recommendation.

TAKE TIME TO INTERVIEW

You will want to interview more than one attorney. You will be working closely with this person, you need to feel comfortable, and it is worth the time and expense. Sometimes lawyers will speak with you over the telephone, but more frequently, you will need to make an appointment and pay for a consultation.

You will want an attorney to explain the law to you. To do this, he or she will need to ask you questions about the marriage. Come prepared to all interviews. Bring a list of your assets and income and expenses to the meeting. That way, you will be able to get the most out of each interview. You can compare what lawyers tell you, analyze who gave you the best information, and determine if the "chemistry" is right. (Although you should never look for a romantic link with your attorney, you should be able to feel comfortable with him or her.) You need to be able to ask questions, trust, and respect this individual. You need to feel that the lawyer will give your case the proper time and thought, will care about your case, and be an effective advocate. If the lawyer continually answers a million other phone calls while speaking with you, consider going elsewhere. The lawyer should give you the time and attention you deserve. Remember, you are paying for his or her service and should be satisfied with what you get.

You should get the proper attention and respect from the lawyer. You also want honesty. If a lawyer spends your time regaling you with stories of how wonderful he or she is and all his or her great wins, think about going elsewhere. You want to choose a person with whom you can work and from whom you can learn the law and your options. Ultimately, you are the person who makes the final decisions. Your lawyer should give you the knowledge and the tools to help you make them.

You should be aware that if you interview an attorney, your spouse may not hire that particular attorney, as it would be a conflict of interest. And likewise, you are not allowed to hire anyone your spouse has interviewed.

A good lawyer is very familiar with judges and masters and knows their biases and quirks. One judge from the Northeast says, "How you prepare your case depends on who your judge is." Lawyers should be very familiar with how judges rule on certain issues. (Note, however, that judges are human beings and have been known to change their minds! They are not totally predictable.) I attended a seminar at which a particular judge gave a list of all the relevant issues she looks for in order of importance. In preparing for a court hearing before that judge, I followed the list and got a very good result. Lawyers should attend continuing legal education classes. Masters (lawyers who hear a case before there is a hearing before a judge) and judges often lecture at these courses. Ask lawyers you are interviewing how many hours of continuing legal education they attend each year.

SHOULD YOU EVER SWITCH LAWYERS?

People find it comfortable to stay with the same lawyer, and if things go well, that's the way it should go. No one wants the trouble and expense of having to get used to someone else as well as start over. Still, you may find that at a certain point you need to change counsel. Don't, however, switch lawyers just because you don't like the advice. Get a second opinion first. Yes, it costs money, but it may be less expensive in the long run for you to get a second opinion and make sure the advice you are getting is sound. It will be even more expensive to start all over. If your second opinion concurs, and you are satisfied with the representation in all other respects, don't switch.

There are times when a change is necessary. Change lawyers if:

- *Your lawyer will not return your phone calls. You must be able to reach your lawyer to ask questions or review material. Lawyers can get busy, but you shouldn't stick with one who is too busy to answer your questions. You may receive a phone call from a secretary or associate explaining that the attorney is in court and can't return your call immediately. That's to be expected. You shouldn't, however, be kept waiting any longer than twenty-four hours. If your matter is an emergency, you should leave a message saying so, and your call should be returned promptly. Remember, though, that you can't call your lawyer and say it's an emergency just because you feel like chatting. That's crying wolf and may have the same effect. If you do this all the time, your lawyer may not return calls that you say are emergencies. Use your judgment. That said, lawyers owe you a duty of returning calls promptly. It is always better to ask a question and avoid a problem later than to not get a question answered and pay a fortune in legal fees to fix the problem.*

- *Your attorney misses deadlines. The laws of civil procedure—the rules that attorneys follow when they file motions, petitions, and other pleadings—specify time limits within which these pleadings must be filed. These time limits must be strictly observed. You may give up your right to file or answer an important part of your case if your attorney fails to meet a deadline. Never stay with an attorney who misses one.*

- *Your attorney is unprepared. You are paying your lawyer to prepare your case. That means listening to what you and opposing counsel may say, reading letters and pleadings that the lawyers for the opposition send, and responding as promptly as necessary. If your lawyer is not responsive to you, does not prepare for meetings or court hearings, and prejudices your case, you need to find someone who will be attentive. Don't allow the lawyer to bully you and tell you it is your fault they were unprepared. Be an educated consumer. Do your homework and make sure this isn't so. Just because people have a JD beside their name doesn't mean they can slide by without doing the work required.*

- *You feel you are unable to communicate with your lawyer, and he or she is dismissive of your opinions. You are in charge of your life. You need to listen to your lawyer's advice, ask questions, and feel that you get satisfactory answers that are logical and well reasoned. That doesn't mean you won't discuss things and have different opinions to review. If you feel your lawyer is just not listening, however, and you feel uncomfortable all the time, think about switching. At the very least, get a second opinion.*

- *You receive bills that can't be explained or nothing is being accomplished, and you can't get a good explanation of why. Divorce negotiations and litigation take much more time than you can imagine. That's partly because you are dealing with emotions. Sometimes, one side in a divorce matter simply doesn't want to end the marriage, and this can be difficult and often hold up negotiations. However, your attorney should be able to give you logical explanations of the discussions between counsel, as well as of any court involvement. But if your case bogs down, and if your lawyer can't explain to you in language you can understand why nothing is happening and you continue to receive large legal bills, you need to find another lawyer.*

If you do switch lawyers, it is always best to line up a new one before firing the old. The transition should be smooth. Make sure your bill is straight and your file is accessible. If you are contesting the original lawyer's bill, you may have difficulty getting your file. You should always be able to get your file—you may have to pay a copying fee—but you should not allow your lawyer to hold your file hostage.

You need to be honest, though. Let's say you are switching lawyers and your first lawyer did a great deal of work for you, and you didn't pay the bill or have a problem with the amount. You may have to go to a fee dispute committee to settle the bill. However, you need to be fair, too. Ask for an itemized bill from the original lawyer for all work still due and owing. Don't let too much time slip by and allow huge bills to pile up and then complain you don't want to pay. No new lawyer will take on a case if he or she sees you just don't like the idea of paying for legal fees that are legitimate.

Take charge of your case. That means keeping on top of bills and the work being done. If you want to be billed weekly or biweekly in a case where a lot of work is being done, request the bill. If you have only so much money and must work within these constraints, then you have an obligation to discuss this with your lawyer. You can't expect a lawyer to work for free. If you have a large amount of money that will come to you in settlement and your lawyer is willing to wait to get his or her fee, that's fine. *Caution:* You need to establish such an arrangement up front. Be honest in your relationship with your lawyer, or it is doomed for failure.

If you do change lawyers, the original lawyer will need to file a withdrawal of appearance with the prothonotary or clerk of court, and your second lawyer will need to enter his or her appearance. Do what's needed to cooperate. If an attorney is willfully withholding your file, you may need to get help. Your new lawyer could possibly give you advice. If not, call the local bar association.

THINGS YOU SHOULD NEVER DO

1. Never sleep with your lawyer while he or she is representing you.

2. Never use the same lawyer as your spouse. Don't fall for the old line—"It will save you money. You really don't need your own lawyer." If you go through mediation, you may use one lawyer to write a mediation memorandum that states the terms to which you and your spouse agree. You should always use your own lawyer to write and/or review any agreement that will be filed with the court.

3. Never sign any agreement or any piece of writing you do not understand. Never allow an attorney to tell you it's "just legal language" and you don't need to understand it. You need to know exactly what you are signing at all times.

4. If you have a family lawyer who has represented both you and your spouse in the past, don't use him or her in a divorce matter. This is a conflict of interest. You both need independent advocates.

REPRESENTING YOURSELF

Sometimes you absolutely cannot afford an attorney. If this is the case, it is generally wise to get at least a consultation with a lawyer. You may have to borrow some money, but it is worth it to get some legal advice to learn your rights. If your spouse has money, a lawyer may be willing to go to court and request attorney's fees. You may stand to lose significant rights if you do not at least consult with a lawyer.

If there is ever a question of domestic violence, you can go to the courthouse and find out how to file an abuse action. You should never tolerate physical violence under any circumstances. The court will generally provide assistance for you.

TAKE TIME TO MAKE CERTAIN THAT YOU ARE DOING THE RIGHT THING

It has probably taken years to get to where you are now. It will also take some time to get out of your marriage and preserve your assets and your credit. Interview a few lawyers. Hire the lawyer with whom you feel you are best able to work and who you believe to be your best advocate. Ask questions. Don't be intimidated. Take time to investigate and to make certain that you have made the right choice.

Chapter Eleven

ALIMONY AND SPOUSAL SUPPORT

Alimony is a term given to the money paid by one spouse to the other for a varying period of time after divorce. Alimony is different and separate from child support. It is money paid to a spouse. In some states, the terms used are *spousal support* or *maintenance*. These words are sometimes used interchangeably. Ask to make certain that there is no distinction between the terms in your state.

Alimony is an issue that generally elicits more questions than answers because there are no set rules for determining the compensation. Good and creative lawyering can make a difference in what you get—or don't get. Alimony is awarded in only about 15 percent of all cases. Be aware that while alimony and equitable distribution are two separate issues, in reality, judges sometimes grant alimony because one spouse did not receive enough in the property division. There are no hard-and-fast rules as to exactly when in the process alimony may be granted. (Alimony awarded during the pendency of a divorce, or the period between separation and divorce, is called alimony pendente lite.) In most states, there are various factors that are considered when determining whether or not alimony is appropriate. The following factors are normally considered by judges or other fact-finders:

- *Length of the marriage*

- *Age of the parties*

- *Physical and emotional health of both parties*

- *Income of both spouses*

- *Earning capacity of each spouse*

- *Standard of living during the marriage*

- *Financial and nonfinancial contributions of both spouses to the marriage*

- *Separate property of either spouse that may be available for support*

- *The amount of money each party makes now and how much each can expect to earn in the future*

- *Fault*

- *Education and work experience*

Alimony is generally given when one spouse earns a great deal more than the other, or when there is a large disparity between the income of one spouse and the income or earning capacity of the other. If one earns a large sum of money and the other spouse stays at home, alimony could be given to equalize their positions.

Whether, when, and how much alimony is granted will depend on the specific facts of each case. It also depends on which jurisdiction you live in and what judge may be deciding your case.

A VIEW FROM THE BENCH

One judge from the Northeast remarks that if one spouse was severely injured in an accident on the way out of the wedding ceremony, he or she would probably by entitled to permanent alimony as long as the injury warranted it. It wouldn't matter that they just tied the knot.

One Midwestern judge opines that alimony is a very difficult issue: "How long a person should receive alimony and how much a person should get are very difficult issues for a judge. It is easier to decide in long-term marriages, but then again, 'long-term' means different things to different people." This judge felt that twelve years was a long-term marriage.

According to the 1998 U.S. Census Bureau data, 23 percent of wives earn more than husbands. According to a 1998 survey by Prudential Securities, 48 percent of these women felt that if they were to divorce they thought it fair to pay alimony to their husbands, and 58 percent of those men felt they deserved alimony. This statistic brings up a good point. Both men and women feel that they should be economically compensated when their marriage ends and they earn less than their spouse.

CONTRIBUTION TO THE MARRIAGE

One of the factors considered in any alimony issue is what each spouse contributed to the marriage. It is very important to tell your lawyer all the relevant facts. Let's say you and your spouse decided that one of you would give up a fast-track career so the other could maintain a high-powered position and the family could have a comfortable lifestyle. Even if the agreement was never written down, tell that to your lawyer. If both of you were professionals but one of you worked part-time while the other made partner in a firm, the difference in positions could be significant at the time of divorce. Not only did the spouse who worked part-time give up salary during the marriage, but by taking a non-tenured or nonpartner-track position, that spouse is far behind careerwise and will need to make up for the lost time. He or she may never be able to make up the lost salary. You may be entitled to compensation for your time out of the job market or for any disparities in earning capacity.

Lorna Wendt, whose former spouse, Gary, was CEO of GE Capital, fought a bitter court battle to assert her right to half of all her husband's assets. She believed that she stood by her husband for thirty-two years, raising the kids, being the perfect corporate wife and mother, and helping her husband climb the corporate ladder. Lorna Wendt believed that her contribution toward the marriage was that of an equal partner. She claimed she made everything work so her husband could do everything he needed in both his business and personal life. Wendt wanted half of all her husband's assets. She believed she deserved half of all his pension benefits and stock options, even the unvested ones. Gary Wendt's position was different. He offered his wife between $8 and $10 million, which he felt would allow her to live comfortably. Lorna felt this represented only 10 percent of their total marital estate. Gary Wendt believed their assets were only worth $20 million. Lorna Wendt felt the estate was worth $100 million. Eventually, the case settled for approximately $20 million. The bottom line is that one spouse who helps the other reach certain career goals may argue that in divorce he or she deserves to be compensated as an equal partner for that help.

CONTRIBUTION AND COMPENSATION

Here are some questions that need to be considered:

- *Was the difference in earning capacity between the spouses created during the marriage?*

- *Did one spouse take a hit in earning capacity because of a spousal agreement or other circumstances in the marriage?*

- *Did one spouse give up a career to take care of children, a child, or a parent with special needs?*

- *Did one spouse give up a career so the other spouse could move whenever his or her job demanded a move?*

- *Did one spouse delay a career?*

These are the types of questions you need to ask. You need to take into consideration all aspects of the contribution to the marriage. When you look at the length of the marriage, you also need to look at the impact the length of the marriage had on the job track or careers of each person. If both spouses are young, one spouse might argue that equitable distribution should satisfy both parties and there should be no need for alimony. But special circumstances may come into play. Because the law in domestic relations continuously changes, it is important to discuss with your lawyer all possible arguments. You may be entitled to more—or less—than you expect. If one or both parties are older, this may also affect questions of alimony. The older a spouse is, the more difficult it will be to retrain or reenter the workplace. (Such arguments may also be used in the property division portion of your case.)

STANDARD OF LIVING

Another factor in considering alimony is the parties' standard of living during the marriage. If you live a very lavish lifestyle during your marriage, you might find that you have to subsidize your spouse's standard of living for a while after marriage. Is your spouse used to winter vacations in warm climates and trips to Europe? Does your spouse have an unlimited budget to do what he or she likes to do? The life you were leading during the marriage will be taken into consideration when deciding the alimony factor after a divorce.

What's a Spouse Worth?

If you suspect your marriage is heading for divorce, you might want to figure out your monetary worth to the marriage. When you think about it, you're really asking for your just compensation in dollars and cents for the time spent in your marriage as well as any lost time from the job market and any lost savings from retirement.

EARNING CAPACITY

Another very difficult issue when it comes to alimony (and child support and equitable distribution), is the question of earning capacity. Earning capacity is the amount of money a fact-finder decides a person should be able to earn in the job market. To make this decision, fact-finders take into consideration factors such as the person's education, training, job history, age, health, intelligence, and skills. If a person has been out of the job market for many years, how much income should a judge determine that person should be able to earn? What type of job could a person get if he or she sought a job? The answer to these critical and important questions often involves a good amount of subjective judgment.

Let's say you have stayed at home to raise children and have never worked. What type of job would your experience at home translate into in the job market? Or let's say have a degree in a certain field but have chosen to work in a job that doesn't fully utilize your educational capabilities. Should a higher level of income be attributable to you?

You need to create a best-case/worst-case scenario. If you haven't worked and you don't want to run out and get a forty-hour-a-week job after you have spent the last twenty years at home, you will need advice on how to present a minimized picture of your earning potential. If you want to get more money from your ex (or the other parent in the case of child support), you may need to paint a rosier picture of his or her job skills.

To make a decision about potential or actual earning power, often the court will appoint a vocational expert—a person trained in evaluating a person's job skills and capabilities to earn a certain level of income—to test a person and testify as to that person's earning capacity. The testing can be extensive and costly. In lieu of expert testimony, some fact-finders will base decisions on readily available information regarding salary ranges of certain jobs in different geographical locations.

If health is an issue, many fact-finders will expect a doctor to come to court to testify on the state of a person's health. Doctors may be thoroughly questioned as to a spouse's medical diagnosis and how that affects his or her ability to work. Other fact-finders may allow the introduction of medical records or affidavits of health professionals rather than live testimony. Some jurisdictions allow videotaped depositions of a doctor's testimony so the deposition (minitrial) can be scheduled at the doctor's convenience. It's best to check with a lawyer to determine how your state and county handle this issue.

Unfortunately, many people spend a small fortune on vocational experts only to find that the judge disagrees with the conclusion and money spent on the expert is wasted. (This is one reason you need a good lawyer who can guide you to useful, relevant experts.)

You Could Be Stuck in Your Job Even If You Hate It!

Earning capacity is an issue when a person with a high-salaried position decides he or she no longer wants to work in that job.

Tom always wanted to be a doctor. He fell in love with his high school sweetheart, Susan, and married her right after college. Susan worked while Tom went through medical school. After his internship, Susan became pregnant and stopped working after the birth of the first of their four children. Susan was happy taking care of the kids and never considered working. But Tom became increasingly more unhappy when his medical practice was purchased by an HMO. He hung in for about five years and came home and announced he was leaving Susan to marry his nurse and take a job as a consultant for half the pay. Susan took Tom to court for alimony and child support. Tom claimed he didn't have to work in a job he hated just so Susan and the kids could live an expensive lifestyle.

The court felt differently. The judge ruled that Tom could not voluntarily take that large a cut in pay. Tom's support order was based on the earnings he received for practicing medicine with the HMO. (It is wise to ask an attorney how similar cases in your jurisdiction have been decided.)

Divorce can face you with this unpleasant truth: Courts can enter your life and rule that you are not free to do what you want.

Under the law, you have a duty to support your children and your spouse in the same standard of living you enjoyed during the marriage. If you lose your job, the case is altered, but voluntarily taking a pay cut won't guarantee that you'll pay less or receive more in spousal or child support.

The facts of each case are different, and the rulings are somewhat subjective. If there are compelling reasons to leave your job, the court may permit lower support due to the salary cut. One lawyer from the Northeast points out that this is an area where a judge's biases may come into play. All may depend on how the facts appear to the judge. A judge may also decide similar cases differently if one person seems credible and sincere and another person rubs him or her the wrong way.

Location, location, location. The sum you receive in alimony may very well depend on where you live.

As Good as It Gets

One lawyer from the Midwest handled a divorce in which one spouse earned a great deal of money and the other spouse did not work. When it came time for alimony, the trial court awarded a very small amount, considering the working spouse's high income—alimony was $1,700/month. On appeal, the appellate court reversed the decision and held that alimony should be $4,700/month. This increase may seem large; however, the marriage was a long one—well over twenty years—and this amount represented only 18 percent of the working spouse's income. The lawyer stated that this case was an example of an alimony award in her state, and that was as good as it gets.

Compare the Law in Wisconsin

When a couple has been married many years the court feels it is reasonable to consider an equal division of total income as the starting point for alimony. What does this mean in dollars and cents? The dependent partner in a marriage may be entitled to 50 percent of the total earnings of both parties as alimony payments. The law in Wisconsin truly seems to be as good as it gets!

SHORT-TERM OR REHABILITATIVE ALIMONY

Sometimes alimony will be awarded for a short period of time so the person receiving it will be able to go back to school for retraining or have some time to reenter the job market. A judge from the Southwest feels that this type of "bridge" or rehabilitative alimony is often a good way to help spouses get back on their feet. Often rehabilitative alimony is used when a person is relatively young and has a relatively long period of time that he or she will be able to be productive. This type of alimony is fact-specific. Look at all the elements of your case. Check with a lawyer in your state.

ALIMONY IS NOT GUARANTEED

Even if you are awarded alimony, there is not an ironclad guarantee you'll actually get your money even if you take all the necessary steps to try to secure and enforce the payments. An alimony award also means you'll be dealing with your spouse for some time to come. Emotionally, you may want to sever all contact with your ex once the divorce is final.

For Payors of Alimony

- *Alimony is tax-deductible for the person paying it.*

- *Alimony is included in the recipient's income.*

- *If the person paying alimony is in a higher tax bracket and the recipient is in a lower tax bracket, the IRS is the party who will suffer the loss! Think of the alimony as a way of saving taxes rather than enriching your spouse.*

If your spouse balks at alimony, maybe you can agree to take a larger amount in the property distribution instead. That's not all bad in every case. At least then you know you have a specific amount of money in your possession. You won't have to depend on the periodic payments to arrive.

Keep in mind that whatever method of property distribution you negotiate, you need to make certain that you at least consider all the issues and all possible alternatives.

If you do choose periodic alimony payments, the IRS demands that certain criteria must be met for payments to be deemed alimony. Careful drafting by a lawyer is critical here.

INTERNAL REVENUE SERVICE GUIDELINES

- *Payments must be made pursuant to a written agreement.*

- *Payment must be made in cash or cash equivalent (check or money order payable on demand) and must be for a specified amount.*

- *Both spouses cannot be living in the same house.*

- *Each spouse must file a separate tax return.*

- *Alimony payments must stop after the death of the person receiving the payments.*

- *For the first three years, payments may not decrease by $15,000 or more from one year to the next. If the payments do, the person paying the alimony would have to pay taxes on all the money deducted from the prior year's taxes.*

You also can stipulate certain provisions that make the alimony provision easier to bear:

- *You can make alimony modifiable so you can increase or decrease the amount depending on changes in income or changes in health.*

- *You can provide that alimony will stop if your ex starts living with a boyfriend or girlfriend or if your ex remarries.*

- *You can provide that the amount of alimony is nonmodifiable. At least that way the amount will never increase.*

- *You can specify the number of years you will pay.*

Alimony can also consist of payment of insurance premiums or mortgage payments. Check with your attorney and a financial/tax consultant to ensure that the terms of the alimony benefit both spouses. If one spouse can make a payment of a high-ticket item and get a tax benefit while the other spouse is benefitted and not harmed by it, everyone wins. Also check to ensure that the language required by the IRS is met. You really can never make paying money to an ex pain-free, but you can make it less painful.

Consider the following scenarios and all the variables that can affect whether or not a person receives alimony:

Case One

Lisa and Jack were married for nine years. Jack is a CEO of a major corporation, and they relocated for his job three times during the marriage. When he was transferred to different locations, Lisa stayed behind and packed up the house. When she arrived at their new location, she would scout around for a house to buy and decorate. Lisa is thirty-two and hasn't worked in eight years. Lisa's vocational skills are minimal. She graduated from high school and went to art school for two years before she began to work. After the marriage, Lisa worked for a year but was not able to find work when they moved. Also, Jack gave her duties that effectively prevented her from working. Jack wanted Lisa available full-time to arrange parties, do charity work with the other spouses, and run errands. In the beginning of their marriage, Lisa also accompanied Jack when he had to travel for business; however, after four years, Jack found it easier to travel alone. He soon became involved with a woman he met along the way.

The fact-finder in this case has to balance Lisa's earning power against any possible compensation for her. Because Lisa is young, she is capable of going back to school to get training so she can earn money. However, Lisa did stay around the house and ensure that Jack could continue to move up in his world. If the property split is fifty-fifty, the fact-finder in this case might add on alimony for Lisa for a certain period of time. Nine years is not considered a short marriage; however, this is not a case in which Lisa would get alimony indefinitely. The court might well decide she was perfectly capable of working, as long as she is healthy and has the ability to get a job, some vocational training, or some education. If Lisa and Jack had children, the situation would be different. If Lisa and Jack had small children, Lisa would probably get alimony for a longer time. However, the decision would depend on the state in which she lived, when they divorced, and the amount of property Lisa received.

Consider another possibility: Let's say Lisa is diagnosed with multiple sclerosis after two years of marriage. Although she is not completely disabled, Lisa tires easily and has trouble walking. Her doctor advises her that it would not be good to have a full-time job or too much stress. The most she should consider working is fifteen to twenty hours a week. The doctor can't predict if the disease will ever become severe enough to render her incapable of working. In this case, Jack might face having to pay Lisa permanent alimony. She should at least receive alimony for a longer time than she would have in the first scenario. The courts would likely reexamine her prognosis periodically. Meanwhile, Jack should require Lisa to inquire as to her job options and possible schooling or training for physically undemanding work she could pursue part-time.

Case Two

Bob and Mary were married for twelve years and had two children. Mary is a doctor, who worked part-time after the kids were born. However, she was given an ultimatum at work: Work full-time or not at all. Mary liked her practice. Bob was a research scientist and he was able to pick up the slack at home. After a few years, Mary found herself with extra shifts and less time at home. Bob did all the carpooling, took the kids to the doctor's, and co-ordinated all their activities. Bob and Mary decided after twelve years that things weren't working out with their marriage. They decided to go to counseling. After a year and a half, they were ready to call it quits. Mary earned significantly more than Bob, who had passed up promotions so he could be at home when the kids needed him.

Mary had enjoyed being at home with the kids, too, but she couldn't say no when faced with a choice between more hours or no hours. In the divorce, Mary received a great shock. Not only did Bob end up with primary custody of the kids and a large sum each month in child support, but Mary also had to pay Bob a nice sum each month in alimony. Had Mary realized she was putting herself in the position of working harder, seeing her kids less, and paying her ex handsomely for staying home, she would have reconsidered her career move while she still had time to do something about it.

Whether or not you receive alimony is very fact-specific and also depends upon where you live. You should, however, consult with a lawyer before making any career changes before, during, and after divorce if you still have to make support payments. You don't want to make a move that you'll later regret.

Chapter Twelve

CHILD SUPPORT

Child support payments are made by the noncustodial parent to the custodial parent to pay for the needs of the children. Child support is not optional; it is mandatory. Child support helps the custodial parent pay for basic living expenses—mortgage, rent, utilities, food, clothing and more. At the very least, child support is intended to help the lesser-earning parent be better able to afford these necessities for the children.

Problems arise when the noncustodial parent thinks they are paying out money that will never be used for the children. What these parents overlook is the expense of running a household. Additionally, they need to purchase duplicate possessions if the child is staying at both parents' homes.

Congress passed the Family Support Act in 1988, which requires all states to adopt a uniform, statewide formula to determine

a baseline or guideline amount of support that the higher-earning
parent generally must pay to the lower-earning parent. You
should check with a lawyer, or at the least your family court
if there are personnel available there to help, to find out how
much money you may be entitled to receive or how much you
can expect to pay. Beware: These are minimum amounts the law
mandates must be paid and should be seen as a guideline only.
There are many variables that make every case different. By using
this minimum number as a starting point, however, you can begin
to determine how much money you might expect to pay or
receive.

HOW ARE GUIDELINE AMOUNTS CALCULATED?

Each state has its own guidelines that are strictly followed to determine how much child support is owed. In some states, only the
income of the parent paying the support and the number of children are considered. In other states, the income of both parents is
factored in. When both incomes are considered, this method is
referred to as "income share formula." Basically, what this formula tries to accomplish is to approximate the amount of money
each parent would spend on their children if they had not divorced. In theory, children shouldn't be penalized financially by
their parents' split. In some states, a percentage of the parents' incomes are allocated for support. Varying percentages of income
may be applied if there is more than one child.

It is an absolute necessity that you learn your state's guidelines.
You can go to a lawyer, your local courthouse, a law library, or
even the web to find your state statute. (A good starting point is
www.law.cornell.edu.) In only exceptional cases should you expect
to pay less than this mandated amount.

If you and your spouse earn in excess of the guideline amount, the courts will determine the amount of support. Consult a lawyer if your case is above the minimum guideline amount. Different states have different ways of figuring support amounts in such cases. In most states, the guideline amount is used as a starting point and then additional needs are added into that figure.

ADDITIONAL NEEDS

Many different variables may enter into the support calculations after a guideline number is set. Certain special needs, such as medical needs and child care, are taken into consideration and may bring the guideline amount up or down. The following are examples of special needs that may apply in your case:

- *Private school tuition*

- *After-school activities such as music or art lessons*

- *Camp or other summer activity*

- *Psychiatric or psychological counseling not provided by medical insurance*

- *Baby-sitting costs*

- *Unusual custody arrangements where children spend well more than half the time with one parent*

- *Private tutoring*

- *Sports equipment and other sport-related expenses*

- *Income of a noncustodial parents' new spouse*

Because each child is different and every family's finances are different, additional needs must be figured on a case-by-case basis. For example, if a child were training for the Olympics, the cost of training, travel expenses, and many other additional expenses would arguably be additional needs.

If you know in advance that one or all your children have certain medical needs—psychological counseling or orthodontic bills—you may want to negotiate in advance how much each parent will contribute toward these bills. Many kids play sports—baseball, football, ice hockey—and the equipment and insurance can be costly. If you know that a child is involved in an activity that costs money and you don't want to shoulder the cost alone, present the numbers to the other parent and decide how to split it. It is less expensive just to pay the bills and skip the attorney fees and court costs for the battle.

When one parent's income is high and far exceeds the guideline amount, additional needs could conceivably include items such as cell phones, cars, horseback riding lessons, and any other luxuries to which a child was accustomed while the parents were together. The reasoning is that the children should be able to enjoy the same standard of living they would have if their parents didn't divorce.

The case law regarding "high-end" cases, or cases in which one parent earns a significant amount of money, differs from state to state and even county to county. Every day courts in different jurisdictions are deciding cases in different ways of how much is too much. The case of Kirk Kekorian—the California businessman with a purported $6.4 million earnings in 2001—is a good example of how one spouse's riches will motivate the other spouse to make rich demands. Lisa Bonder Kerkorian, a former women's pro tennis player who retired in 1988, requested $320,000 a month for her three-year-old daughter. Among the purported requested needs of her child were $144,000 for travel expenses and play dates, $7,000 for charity, $102,000 for food, and the list went on and on. As you can see, one side's claims about what are reasonable additional needs can be rather inventive. It really is necessary to find out what the courts in your state have ruled in similar cases.

HOW LONG ARE YOU REQUIRED TO PAY CHILD SUPPORT?

States require that child support be paid until a child reaches the age of majority. Generally that means eighteen years of age, the age of graduation from high school, or twenty-one years of age, but check your state law. If you have a disabled child, you may be responsible for paying child support for as long as the child remains a dependent. Your obligation may end if your child gets married or joins the military. Certain states require parents to pay for a child's college education; others do not.

If you are agreeing to pay a certain amount of child support, consider including in your negotiation the exact duration for which the support will be paid. If you know you are going to have problems in the future communicating with the other parent, you might consider dotting all the i's and crossing all the t's in your agreement. You and your lawyer must be very careful.

A lawyer in North Carolina tells of a case in which she stipulated in a property settlement agreement that child support would be paid until the child reached the age of eighteen. The agreement was written when the child was six. The child turned eighteen during the first few months of her senior year in high school. The lawyer had assumed that the child would be eighteen upon graduation from high school. The parent refused to continue to pay support, the child was now unsupported for part of the senior year, the parent with custody cried foul, and the case went back to court.

Don't make any assumptions. (Your lawyer shouldn't, either.) If you expect support to be paid until a child graduates from high school, say it specifically in the agreement. Courts don't like to give away a child's right to support, but not all states permit later modifi-

cations of agreements. Being careful when you make the agreement is a good way to avoid going back to court in the future, which is always a good idea.

BE SPECIFIC IN YOUR SUPPORT ORDER OR AGREEMENT

If you have more than one child, you should state how much each child is receiving and until what age. If you are not specific in detail, you may find yourself in a position where one child reaches the age of majority but the person paying the support will still have to pay the full amount as if the child were still a minor. If you have a support order for $500 every two weeks for two children, you may find that you will be stuck paying the same amount for one child. And don't expect support for two children to necessarily double the amount for one child. It could be more. Depending on your income level and the state you live in, you will probably find that the amount of support for each child increases in percentage increments. Therefore, if you are paying $1,000 for two children, you may find that you will pay $800 for one child after the first child reaches the age of majority. Check state guidelines or consult with an attorney. Avoid court later on: Spell out exactly how many children are included in the support order and until what age. (In some cases it may work to your advantage to be less specific. If your lawyer has a good reason to write a more general provision, you may want to follow that advice.)

GROSS INCOME OR NET INCOME

There is a distinction between these two ways of figuring income. Gross income represents your entire income without taking any deductions for such things as taxes. Net income is generally determined by subtracting your federal, state, and Social Security taxes as well as any Medicare deductions. Most states use net income when determining the amount of child support owed. Health insurance is treated differently in different states: Sometimes it is deducted, sometimes not. There may be other allowable deductions such as union dues or mandatory retirement payments. The general guideline is that if the deductions are mandatory rather than voluntary, they will be subtracted from your gross paycheck. Check with an attorney or your state statutes to figure out how your jurisdiction determines this issue.

If you are a wage earner who receives W-2 income, your net income is relatively easy to figure out. However, if you or your spouse is self-employed, it is more difficult. In that case, you may need the help of an accountant. You must review all the factors (discussed in Chapter Three) that constitute income, such as the costs and expenses paid for by the business, and perks and additional bonuses or compensation. If certain expenses are paid for by your employer or your business—such as the cost of a company car or entertainment expenses—those expenses may be added into the amount the courts will consider to be part of your income. An accountant and your lawyer should be able to help you with these calculations.

Bonuses, inheritances, and money from overtime or second jobs may be included in your income. When figuring out child support, think about any extra money either you or your spouse may receive from any source. Check to see how your state handles and characterizes incomes such as these. Sometimes, in the middle of a divorce process but before the settlement, a spouse, strapped for cash, may decide to take on a second job just to pay the bills. But such a move might have bad consequences down the line. A master or fact-finder, when determining your income as a basis for future child support payments, may see the extra income, include it in your total income, and order a child support payment that will have you working eighty-hour weeks for years. So before accepting extra work or income, consult with your lawyer or financial adviser to make sure it won't come back to bite you. You may find yourself stuck working three jobs if you divorce whether or not you want to!

As with determining alimony, an income can be imputed to you even if you do not work. Usually, in many states, once a child is of school age and a parent's presence at home is not as critical—nor do you have to basically use your salary just to pay day-care expenses—the court may rule that a parent is able to work and will consider education, skill, background, and all the other pertinent factors on which to determine the amount of money you could be capable of earning if you did work.

HOW DOES SHARED CUSTODIAL TIME AFFECT CHILD SUPPORT?

Custodial arrangements have changed away from the traditional arrangement in which Mom maintained primary custody and Dad more or less just saw the kids every other weekend. Now courts recognize the need to take into consideration the actual time the child spends with each parent. That shift, in turn, forced states to review their support guidelines. The courts recognize that it is in a child's best interest to have frequent contact with each parent; therefore, the law is continually being reviewed concerning adjustments in child support payments when children spend a great deal of time—in some cases equal time—with both parents.

In some states you can have a fifty-fifty arrangement, in which children spend equal time with each parent, and still not have the child support reduced. In some states, under this fact pattern, no child support would be due and owing. The variations are great.

If you and your soon-to-be-ex are spending equal or close to equal time with children, you should contact a lawyer to see what impact your custodial arrangements may have on your child support.

When deciding how much time you spend with a child, courts generally consider the number of overnights a child has with each parent. Therefore, if you have your child spend an evening with you but take the child back to the other parent at bedtime, you will probably not get "credit" for the night. This may not be an ideal way to determine who gets credit; however, if it is the standard used by the courts, you will have to deal with it. Again, this area of the law will most probably continue to change as custody arrangements change.

Custody and support are considered separate issues by the court. However, in real life, they are not. One parent often will threaten to "go for full custody" so that he or she will frighten the other parent into withdrawing their request for child support. This is an area that really requires adults to be mature and decide what is truly in a child's best interest. You may be able to figure out what compromises you are willing to make for an amount of child support with which you can live.

DO I NEED TO PAY SUPPORT IF MY CHILD IS WITH ME FOR SUMMER VACATION?

Let's say you are paying support to the other parent who lives in a different state and has custody of your child. You and the other parent have agreed that the child will spend summers with you. Now, it may not seem fair to you, but, in addition to paying for everything your child needs while staying with you for the summer, you must continue to send child support payments to the other parent—you have to pay them unless you get a written agreement otherwise. (Such agreement should be filed with the court.) The rationale behind support is that you are defraying costs of a child living in the other parent's house, and those costs will exist whether the child is there or is temporarily absent.

If a child is in another state and incurs additional expenses such as camp or baby-sitting costs, the parent who does not have physical custody also may have to pay a percentage of the additional costs. You should check with a lawyer if you have questions.

COLLEGE EXPENSES

The law varies from state to state on a parent's responsibility to pay for higher education. Some states require parents to pay for college. The law in other states specifically state that parents are not responsible to pay a penny toward their child's college education. If you think your child will want to attend college or vocational training after high school, you may want to negotiate a minimum level of support or a portion of the expenses each parent will pay.

Check the law in your state. You may also want to get advice from your lawyer to see if there is an "unwritten" law. A lawyer from Florida says if a couple can afford college tuition, it is best to try to address the issue and include it in a property settlement agreement. This lawyer felt it is an unwritten rule that judges will try to include college expenses in a property agreement when a couple is capable of paying for college. The judge wants to know that the college expenses are prepaid or will be paid. The reasoning is that a child whose parents can afford to pay for college should not be penalized if the parents choose to divorce. In some states, however, the courts refuse to intervene and make a parent pay for college expenses.

HOW TO ENFORCE A SUPPORT ORDER

In January 1994, the federal government passed certain laws to streamline rules and procedures regarding the collection and enforcement of child support. All states were given the power to order employers to deduct automatically the amount of a child support order from the obligors or payer's paycheck. So if you have a child support order, you have the right to have the amount of child support deducted from your ex-spouse's paycheck. The employer can send the money into the proper administrative branch of the family court. The court can then mail the money to you. This may take longer than having your ex send the money directly to you, but this method gives you a certain power of enforcement and assures that you will get the money if your ex is still receiving a paycheck.

If, however, the parent paying support is self-employed, enforcing child support may be more difficult. In this situation, the parent owing support should send a check to the court or other administrative agency, which processes the check. State procedures may vary. However, most states provide that checks can be sent to a court-mandated facility that will then send the payment to you. Check the procedure in your state.

If the obligor or payer of support does not work but receives a pension or other benefits, it is possible to have the administrator of that pension plan deduct the child support amount from the periodic payments. (A QDRO can also be used to segregate child support payments. Refer to the box on QDROs in Chapter Six.)

If your child support payments go through the family court system and you do not receive the money, there are certain enforcement procedures you can take advantage of:

- *IRS intercept. This is a program that gives the Internal Revenue Service power to intercept or take any tax refunds owed to the payer and send it to the recipient of the child support payment.*

- *You can place a lien on the payer's property and force a sale of the property. There are different procedures in each state. The lien will prevent a parent from selling property until the support is paid, or force a sale of the property so you can get the money owed. Check your state laws and rules.*

- *Contempt hearings. You can file a petition in court when a parent fails to pay child support. Judges have been known to throw the parent who refused to pay in jail.*

- *Some states will refuse to renew a payer's driver's license or professional license. Some states have put a "boot" on a deadbeat's car. This may seem counterproductive because a parent might need a car to drive to work, but it has been effective in getting parents to pay!*

- *There are provisions for reporting delinquents to a National Registry for New Hires so if a parent who doesn't pay gets a new job, the new employer can be contacted.*

- *You can get bank accounts frozen until the support is paid. Some delinquents have been known to pay so they can use their ATM card again.*

The federal government is serious about helping parents get the child support they need. The enforcement resources available make it compelling for any parent owed child support to register support orders with the court. (Registering an order is filing that order with the clerk in the county and state in which it will be enforced.) You can't use the enforcement remedies available to you unless the system has the court order on record.

If parents live in different states, there are federal laws designed to help enforce support orders. The Uniform Reciprocal Enforcement of Support Act (URESA) and the Uniform Interstate Family Support Act (UIFSA) provide enforcement help for parents who may live in one state with children while the other parent lives and works in a different state. You may be able to file an enforcement action in the state in which you live. (That will eliminate travel expenses to another state in order to collect the support.)

CAN I PROVIDE FOR DIRECT PAYMENT OF THE CHILD SUPPORT?

Some people prefer to have a support check sent directly to them or provide for the payment to be deposited into a joint or other type of checking account. Be aware that if you do so, you may not be able to take advantage of all the enforcement techniques. (When you have an order registered and there are missed payments, the computer system should register those missed payments and automatically begin the enforcement proceedings. Without a registered order, there is no record of missed payments. If you do have a written support agreement, you will have to go into court and sue on the breach of the agreement.) If you do decide you want to have support paid directly to the other parent, take certain precautions:

Never pay cash! If you are the person paying the support, you will always want to be able to produce the canceled check so you can provide evidence that you have paid the support.

Remember that paying support is separate and apart from buying clothing and other necessities. You cannot subtract from your support payment the amount of money you paid for any necessities you may buy for the child, such as food, clothing, or school supplies. Child support is the amount you pay the other parent to help that person provide necessities. You are paying support because you are earning more money. Conversely, the parent receiving the support is supposed to use that money to pay for a child's or children's needs.

CAN AN ORDER BE CHANGED?

Child support orders are subject to change. If you are the noncustodial parent, you might ask for a change of support for any of the following reasons:

- *A decrease or loss of income*

- *A reasonable increase in expenses—not "needing" a new sports car*

- *A substantial change in income by the custodial parent such as a bonus, inheritance, or other newly acquired income*

- *A change in your children's needs*

If you are the custodial parent, you may ask for a change in support for any of the following reasons:

- *A decrease in income that is not a voluntary decrease*

- *Reasonable increased expenses, which may include medical bills, or a need (if both parents agree) for a child to attend a special needs school or private school*

- *Changes in the noncustodial parent's income, such as a substantial increase in salary, winning the lottery, a major inheritance, or acquisition of any income-producing property*

It always pays to keep track of your expenses. You may want to start a file for receipts regarding purchases made for your children. Some parents like to use a computer program that can track expenses from month to month. Remember that it is always best to back up any statements of expenses with the actual receipts of the items purchased. This way, you always have records if you need them.

Tax Considerations

- *Child support is not taxable to the person who receives it, nor deductible by the person who pays it.*

- *A custodial parent may file as head of household on a tax return.*

- *If you are the custodial parent, you are presumed to be paying more than one-half of the support for your child, and you may take a dependency exemption for the children. If you are the custodial parent but negotiate for your ex to claim this exemption, you will need to file a form 8332 with the IRS. (Depending on your tax bracket, it may be beneficial to allow the other parent to take the exemption. Check with a tax adviser and review with your lawyer what the impact on the support calculations will be. You might even negotiate for slightly more support instead of taking the exemption.) You can sign this form on a yearly basis and leave your options open from year to year.*

- *If you are primary custodian, you may be eligible for a child-care credit.*

- *A child of divorced parents is treated as a dependent of both parents for purposes of the medical expense deduction. Expenses paid by either parent can be included as medical expenses on that parent's tax return.*

- *It is wise to have an expert review both parents' tax returns to determine what credit, deductions, and exemptions may have been taken that could affect the numbers used as net income. It can save you money in the end.*

Keep in mind that there are computer programs available to compute support. You may want to consult a lawyer to make certain all the necessary variables are plugged into any software program you may use.

CUSTODY AND SUPPORT

Although custody and support are two different issues, in reality they are always intermingled. It never seems to fail that when one parent files for a change in custody, a petition for a modification in support follows.

Mike and Jane were married for seven years. Mike is a salesman. Jane is a nurse's assistant. They have two children, Tim and Tom, ages five and seven. After a huge fight one evening, Mike moved out of the marital home and said he wanted a divorce. Jane's major concern was her kids. She worked in a doctor's office, generally from 8 A.M. until 4 P.M. Her mother helped out with baby-sitting while Jane worked. However, five months after Tom left, Jane was told she had to work some evening shifts. At first, Jane asked Mike to help out. She found it difficult to pay all the bills, so she filed a petition for child support.

When Mike received the petition, he went ballistic. "No way will I give *you* anything. If you can't pay for the kids, I'll get custody." Jane was scared to death. She was concerned that her late hours at work would allow Mike to gain custody of the children. She really needed the money to pay bills. Jane went to a lawyer. In the end, Jane's lawyer and Mike's lawyer worked out an agreement. However, before Jane sought legal advice, she was ready to borrow money from her mom rather than ask for the child support.

It is not unusual for one parent to threaten a custody suit. Although child support and custody are two separate issues, as you can see by this example, a request for child support (or a request for an increase in an existing support order) often triggers a threat to "get custody" of the kids. Seek legal advice to discuss this matter.

In sum, child support is not optional. Every parent owes a duty of support to his or her children. At the very least, you should check the support guidelines in your state. You need to determine your family's monthly income. Next, you need to make a list of your expenses and any of your children's special needs. See if your custody arrangement will in any way affect your child support. If your family income is above the monthly guideline amount, you might want to get legal help. Make certain that any written agreement is specific and enforceable. Make certain, too, that any tax advantages are fairly split between parents. Whether you should receive child support is not negotiable. It is a child's right.

Chapter Thirteen

TO FIGHT OR NOT TO FIGHT?

Should you fight to the finish in court? Or should you settle the issues in your divorce with the help of a lawyer or mediator or by one of the other alternative dispute resolution methods? Most divorce cases—approximately 80 to 90 percent—settle before going to trial. One compelling reason is that fighting is expensive. It is also emotionally debilitating and often counterproductive. Pursuing alternative routes is less costly in every way.

Before you decide which route to take, you need, once again, to organize your financial information and get a grasp on the issues involved. Next, you and your spouse must both be willing to agree to negotiate rather than fight. Sometimes one party wants to negotiate and the other won't agree. Your strategy may well depend on whether opposing counsel advises your spouse to escalate the war.

DECIDE WHAT YOU NEED

Whatever route you ultimately choose, it is a wise choice to get an initial consultation with a lawyer.

The lawyer's role is that of an advocate who will tell you your rights and obligations. It is essential that you know what money you might be entitled to and the type of distribution you could conceivably receive. True, no one can guarantee what your ultimate property split will be if you go to court. Lawyers can, however, tell you the law, your state guidelines for support payments, and an idea of whether or not you are entitled to alimony or spousal support payments or whether you will be making these payments.

If you don't have money to pay for a lawyer, gather all the financial material, write down all your questions, and save enough money to get a consultation. Unless abuse is an issue and your safety is at stake, it may be wise to put off a divorce and save up until you can get the advice you need. You should know what your rights and obligations are. If you don't, you can't negotiate effectively, and it could cost you more in the end.

Once you know your rights, there is the question of strategy. Because court fights can get very expensive, you may find that you will spend more on lawyer's fees than you will ultimately get from a court battle. There are effective alternatives to going to court.

MEDIATION

Mediation is a method of dispute resolution in which you and your divorcing spouse use the skills of a third person to help you negotiate and reach a financial settlement on some or all the issues.

A mediator's role is different from a lawyer's role. Mediators may begin with an overview of the basic divorce law. However, a mediator is not a hired advocate. The role of a mediator is that of a neutral third party. The hope is that this person can help you and your soon-to-be-ex listen to each other's positions and eventually come up with a compromise on your own. Mediators try to achieve a win-win situation in which each spouse gets some of the things they want. (Some mediators are, by the way, lawyers, but they do not wear the "lawyer's hat" during mediation.)

A trained mediator will help you communicate your concerns to your spouse. True, many marriages end because of lack of communication, but divorce mediation actually promotes spousal communication one last time. In the best of situations, mediation teaches you how to listen effectively to your spouse so you are able to work out disputes later on. On support matters, mediators address the issues of what you "need" to live and what you consider to be necessary extras. They can also help you review your assets and their valuations so you can split your property and your debt.

When it comes to economic issues, mediators try to get the parties to focus on what they need to live and how best to share the money—especially when kids are involved. Through a process of presenting your concerns and needs and listening to your spouse's concerns and needs, you bargain for an agreed-upon settlement. You may also discover some effective tools for communication with your ex. (If you have no children, you may never need to contact your spouse after the divorce. However, you may find that the negotiation techniques you learn may be helpful in your job or other areas of your life.)

In attempting to reach a settlement, the language of mediators differs from the language of lawyers. They use the words *needs, concerns, interests,* and *equalization* or *sharing income.* Many mediators dislike the use of the word *entitlement.* It's not productive to plead your case by saying, "I'm entitled to a nice car and a health club membership and . . ." They tire of hearing "I want!" Many mediators feel that couples should focus on how much money they need to live and then, perhaps, add in those reasonable additional amounts that are in keeping with your standard of living throughout the marriage. One mediator from Pennsylvania finds that when couples determine what money they need for child support, including any special or additional needs or concerns, the dollar amount usually comes fairly close to what the guidelines in support recommend. Mediators don't want couples to be greedy, just realistic.

Contact the Association for Conflict Resolution or ACR (202-667-9700) or check the website (www.acresolution.org) to get names of mediators in your state. ACR is a merged organization of the American Academy of Family Mediators, The Conflict Education Network, and the Society of Professionals in Dispute Resolution. Other organizations you may contact are The American Bar Association (www.abanet.org; 312-988-5000) and the Association of Family and Conciliation Courts or AFCC (www.afccnet.org; 608-664-3750). As with shopping for a lawyer, you should interview several prospective mediators. Ask around. Word of mouth can be a good first lead. You must be cautious, though. There is no licensing required to become a mediator. Experienced mediators go through a training program. Some programs are more rigorous than others. Some mediators have *no* training.

Interviewing Prospective Mediators

Here are some questions you may want to ask a mediator to determine his or her background:

- *What is your educational background?*

- *What degrees do you hold, and what advanced training have you received?*

- *Do you belong to any professional organizations?*

- *How much experience in mediation do you have?*

- *Do you use experts regularly? What type? Do you make referrals?*

- *Are you willing to work with an attorney?*

- *Do you require spouses to mediate in the same room, or do you caucus? (Some mediators will "caucus"—that is, have each spouse sit in a separate room and shuttle back and forth between them. This is sometimes effective if the parties cannot negotiate face-to-face. However, some mediators dislike this method.)*

- *How do you bill? What is your hourly rate?*

- *Do you require a retainer? How much?*

- *Will you send out a written fee agreement detailing your costs and your goals for the mediation?*

If you are only dividing property, you may want to choose a mediator with a financial background. If children are involved and custody is at issue, you may want a mediator with a psychology or social work background. You may find a lawyer who acts as a mediator with experience in both disciplines. It pays to do some research.

Some mediators view their role as a facilitator, or someone who will help you reach a settlement. Other mediators view their roles as evaluators—a third party who will analyze and evaluate your case and dictate the outcome. This type of mediation is more akin to arbitration. If you want someone to help you reach a settlement, you might want a facilitator. If you want someone who is more likely to take charge and push you toward an outcome, you might want to choose an evaluative mediator.

Mediation does require you to negotiate directly with your spouse and to be your own advocate. Therefore, ask yourself some questions before you try to mediate:

- *Am I emotionally and psychologically capable of negotiating face-to-face with my spouse? Am I strong enough to get what I need, or will my spouse intimidate me?*

- *Do I understand my financial picture well enough to bargain for a good settlement?*

- *Can I competently communicate my position to my spouse and to the mediator?*

- *Am I sufficiently over my anger and unemotional enough to listen to and hear what the mediator and my spouse will say?*

Because a mediator's job is different from a lawyer's, you will not have the same relationship with a mediator. However, you should feel comfortable with and be able to communicate with the mediator, and you need to be able to voice your concerns.

Generally, no one walks away from mediation or alternative dispute resolution feeling as if he or she has conquered the other. But your goal in mediation is not to destroy and conquer. If you prepare for mediation by learning your rights, you may be able to decide you don't need to get everything and you can give up certain things you may be entitled to for the sake of getting what you need and feel is fair. Your goal in mediation is to walk away with a settlement that meets your needs while still being able to communicate with your soon-to-be-ex-spouse.

How Much Does Mediation Cost?

Fees for mediation vary. If a mediator is a lawyer, he or she may charge the same fee per hour for mediation as for lawyering. Some attorneys will charge less because their administrative costs are often less for mediation. Experience will probably dictate cost. Fees range from $100 to more than $350 an hour.

Benefits of Mediation

Mediation is often less expensive than using lawyers to settle or litigate your issues, partly because you and your spouse will split the mediator's hourly fee. Mediation can take less time than litigation. If you can gather your information without having to go through legal channels—discovery, including written interrogatories, depositions, and motions in court to produce documents—you will save a great deal of money. There is an easier way of doing things and a more complicated way, and in many cases mediation is an easier way.

Further, if you fight over every detail and request, you will end up paying more money than you can imagine. Mediation can let you be more in control of the issues in your case and help to prevent the case from escalating.

Perhaps the greatest advantage of mediation is that it can bypass the complicated legal process. If you choose to fight in court, you cannot expect a "quick" divorce. Going to court takes time. Your lawyer may file a motion or other request for a hearing. The court will give you a hearing date from weeks to months away. In many counties, there is no unified court system—a system whereby one judge is assigned to hear all aspects of your case. For example, you may file a divorce action in which you request property distribution, support, and custody. If your county does not provide for one judge to hear all these actions of your case, you will have to spend time educating each different judge about your case. This process can get time-consuming and costly. When you are in mediation, you have more control over your case. You are better able to determine how much time it will take to get your divorce.

Fighting can sometimes take on a life of its own. Once you start the fight, you tend to keep fueling the fire. Sometimes when you fight it out you find that you are so intent on jockeying for your position that you get stuck with things you don't even want. How many times have you found yourself arguing with your spouse for something you don't care about but decide to fight for because you know your spouse wants it?

Sometimes people find that they want to use an expert to help them with the mediation. You may feel that you lack the financial sophistication to argue your case. For example, if you are dividing property, you may find that using a mediator but taking a financial expert in with you to help you with complex or confusing financial information or to crunch numbers is the best course of action. And sometimes bringing the right expert in can help cut the expense by efficiently organizing and explaining the financial matters and their impact on your standard of living. Some mediators will not allow the expert to accompany you to the mediation sessions, so you need to ask going into the mediation whether the expert can attend the mediation session.

The Property Settlement Agreement

Even if you decide to go to mediation, you should have a lawyer draw up the property settlement agreement. Your mediator will probably prepare a memorandum of understanding clearly stating what you have agreed to during the mediation. Your lawyer or your spouse's lawyer should then prepare the agreement. You can decide with your spouse which lawyer should prepare the settlement agreement. However, each spouse must have his or her own personal lawyer review the agreement to make certain that all the clauses that are necessary to protect each individual are in place.

ARBITRATION

Arbitration is a dispute resolution process in which you and your spouse go before one person—many times a retired judge—who will listen to both sides of the case and will make a decision for you. In this process, your lawyer will attend the arbitration and be your advocate. Unlike mediation, you do not have to argue your case. Arbitration is a choice when the parties are unable to come up with a settlement on their own and want a third party to make the ultimate decision for them. Arbitration can be structured in a way that can save time and money.

The major difference between mediation and arbitration is that in mediation you and your spouse use the help of a third party to reach your own agreement through negotiation. In arbitration, you give up the ultimate control of the decision to a third party. Sometimes, couples start with mediation and are unable to complete the process. Faced with the choice between a full-fledged court battle or an arbitrator, some couples choose arbitration as a less-hostile and often less-expensive alternative.

The actual arbitration hearing is less formal than a court hearing. Another benefit to arbitration is that you have more control over the timing. It is generally easier to have a hearing scheduled before an arbitrator than before a judge.

Arbitration can be binding or nonbinding. Binding arbitration means that you are stuck with the results whether you like them or not. Nonbinding arbitration means that one or both parties can appeal the outcome.

You might ask an attorney for a recommendation. Many lawyers are not arbitrators, but they may give you the names of competent arbitrators in your area. In addition, try calling your local bar association.

Arbitrators may charge hourly, for a half-day, or a daily rate. This fee varies according to the arbitrator's background and your locale. A retired judge may charge more than a lawyer. As with all other experts, it is always best to ask how much an arbitrator charges in an initial interview.

THE COLLABORATIVE LAW OPTION

Collaborative law is an alternative dispute process dedicated to avoiding court. This process began in California, and the concept is spreading to other states. Presently, there are collaborative law organizations in many states. In a collaborative law process, each spouse has an attorney to represent their interests. Husband and wife and their attorneys sign a contract, called a Collaborative Law Participation Agreement, in which all parties pledge not to go to court. If the process does not work, the attorneys must withdraw and can no longer represent the parties. This practice ensures that lawyers hired in collaborative law cases are there for the sole purpose of negotiating a settlement.

In this case, everyone's energy is channeled toward solving problems and negotiating a settlement. Lawyers for both sides participate with the goal of representing their clients' interests—but they are also trained to listen and appreciate the other side's needs and concerns. The process is geared toward understanding both parties' points of view. This process is akin to mediation, however, unlike mediation, each party can have an attorney by his or her side every step of the way. This practice can be an advantage, especially if one party feels intimidated by the other.

The process runs on the principle of trust. One of the prerequisites is that if one party's lawyer discovers that his or her client has not been honest or candid, that lawyer must shut down the process. Granted, it may be difficult to determine if someone is not being truthful. However, the process runs on the principle that both sides have fully and fairly disclosed all necessary financial information. The final outcome is predicated on this complete and honest disclosure. If, at any point, either party uncovers assets that have not been disclosed, the process ends. That's where doing your homework can help in assessing the other side's honesty.

Each party does rely on a lawyer's advice and guidance. Both parties and lawyers participate in all meetings. The lawyers are, therefore, able to help strategically guide the meetings toward the mutual goal of gathering the necessary information, synthesizing that information, and helping the parties reach a settlement.

If experts are needed, one expert is used, not two. If there is a home that needs to be appraised, you can get one appraisal and reduce the cost. If you need a financial planner to help you figure out how to pay for your children's expenses, both spouses can work with a single planner together to figure out the daunting task of paying for your kids' medical, psychological, dental, and educational expenses. Because you will always have the role of father and mother, this process may enable you to be a better, more informed caretaker for your kids in the future.

One downside to collaborative law is that if the process breaks down, the lawyers cannot continue to represent you. In addition, not all material "discovered" through the process can be used. You may have to spend more money and time getting the same information. But such risks may provide impetus to make the process work. The cost of collaborative law can get expensive because you do pay for your lawyer's time at meetings. But if you use the time wisely, you may find that you can actually cut your costs.

One lawyer in Texas states that one of the major benefits of collaborative law is that—if the lawyers do it right—they will train the parties in nonadversarial techniques of negotiation. As with mediation, this process helps the parties be better able to communicate with one another, which is really a plus if there are children involved.

THE COST OF A COURT BATTLE

One thing is certain: A court battle will cost you more than you can afford in every way. Emotionally, nothing is more devastating than going through a long, drawn-out divorce. One court hearing where you take the witness stand will be one hearing too many. There are times, however, when you absolutely cannot avoid going to court, so try to exhaust all possibilities of settling out of court before you step foot in a courtroom.

Economically, a court hearing is costly because it is extremely time-consuming. For every hour spent in the courtroom, you and your attorney will be putting in hours of preparation time. You should never enter a courtroom unless you are fully prepared, because one misstatement can end up costing you a great deal of money. Further, you need to be emotionally as well as substantively prepared. Losing your temper on the stand can also be costly. You need to know what to say as well as how to say it. Lawyers on television can make court work seem easy, but in the real world, it is anything but.

During the court process, both sides will file documents referred to as "pleadings." Generally, the first pleading to be filed is the divorce complaint. (In some cases, a complaint for support might be the first pleading. Check your state law to determine if you can file for support without filing for divorce. You may want to ask a lawyer to determine if there is an advantage to filing for one and not the other.) These formal documents requesting relief and filed with the court—and many times asking for court intervention—are pleadings.

The person who files the divorce complaint is called the plaintiff. The person against whom the complaint is filed is the defendant. If a motion or petition is filed, the person filing this pleading is referred to as the petitioner. The person who must answer this pleading is the respondent. Check with the clerk of court or your lawyer to determine the cost of filing each pleading. Each state, and the counties within each state, may charge differing amounts.

During the course of the divorce, your lawyer may need to find out answers to questions that he or she is unable to get from your spouse or your spouse's lawyer. This fact-finding is the "discovery" process in which each spouse's lawyer does the work necessary to find out or "discover" the facts of the other spouse's property and income, the total value of those holdings, and other relevant information. In some states, you can pursue discovery without asking the court's permission; in other states, you have to petition the court and request what information you are seeking and why. Depending on how much court intervention is necessary can determine just how costly the process will be.

Discovery also includes questions called "interrogatories." These are questions posed to the other spouse—through the attorneys if the spouse has one—that must be answered within a certain number of days. You will have to pay for your attorney's time to draft the questions. If you need to answer interrogatories sent to you, your lawyer should review your answers.

Sometimes lawyers find it necessary to take the deposition of a spouse or other witness. A deposition is a mini-hearing. Generally, you will attend with your lawyer, who will ask questions of whatever witness is summoned. The witness is generally represented by his or her own lawyer. Lawyers use depositions as fact-finding missions. If you think your spouse is hiding income, your lawyer may ask questions about your spouse's lifestyle, tax returns, business records, or any other relevant information to discover what assets or income your spouse may be trying to keep secret. Depositions generally take place before trials. A day of grueling questioning is sometimes enough to persuade a party to be more cooperative! Anyone connected with the divorce may be called—the spouses themselves, experts for either side, business associates, and any other relevant parties. There will be a stenographer at a deposition or a person transcribing what is being said. (In some states, there may be electronic audio transcription. Sometimes a lawyer will take a video deposition. Ask your attorney if there is any strategic advantage to this.) You will pay for your lawyer's time and for the cost of the notes of testimony when they are transcribed. Check with your attorney for the fee schedule.

Another possible encounter with the court might be a hearing before a master. A master is generally a lawyer who may be selected by court administrators to hear certain issues in divorce cases. For instance, some states have masters who decide property distribution or support issues. In that case, both spouses and their counsel will go before the master. Testimony is presented, and the master will make a decision. In most cases, if you are not satisfied with the result, you can appeal the decision to a judge. Remember, this gets expensive!

Keep in mind that you will be paying for your lawyer's time before the master in addition to the lawyer's time for preparation and time for preparing you. Do not decide that you can just get up and tell your story. Answering questions in court is an art form. You need to learn how to listen to the question and carefully answer only the question asked. This can be quite time-consuming and costly. At the very least, your attorney should role-play, have you take the witness stand, and take you through both direct examination—where your attorney asks you questions—and cross-examination—in which opposing counsel questions you. A rigorous cross-examination should give you a small dose of the real thing.

A more formal hearing or a trial before a judge will take place in a courtroom. A judge and a court reporter will be present. You, your spouse, and any other relevant witnesses such as experts will generally testify. Some trials or hearings can take days; some will last for shorter periods of time.

The rules of litigation—the rules of evidence—apply in a courtroom. Rules of evidence are the formal rules that must be followed when asking and answering questions. You can tell the court only what you know. It is unacceptable to tell the court what someone might have told you or something that you overheard. You can't just blurt out what you want the court to know.

A court hearing can get quite expensive. You pay for your lawyer's time in court, and in addition, you'll pay for all preparation time—whether it is preparing you to testify, preparing witnesses, or writing briefs or trial memoranda. Be prepared to pay a large legal bill.

Keep in mind: Going to court is akin to playing Russian roulette. You have no idea what will happen.

> ▪ *Once you go to court, you put yourself at the mercy of a judge or other fact-finder. In essence, you hand over the decision-making and control of the case to one person. Granted, your lawyer should prepare the case so that the issues are clearly defined for the court. However, once your case is before the court, the judge has the power to request further information or to decide the matter on an issue you may not feel is the most critical or most relevant to your case.*

> ▪ *When you are on the witness stand, you are subject to cross-examination. Your spouse's lawyer may upset you, and you may say things that are detrimental to your case.*

Sally claimed that she could earn only $10,000 a year because she had never worked a day in her life, was a stay-at-home mom, and was fifty years old. She spent all her free time decorating the family homes. When she finished decorating those, she started decorating friends' homes. She considered decorating her hobby. But she felt she really could never work outside the home and earn a living. She said she needed 65 percent of all the marital property and alimony for life so she could continue her lifestyle.

Then Sally was questioned by her husband's lawyer about her "decorating hobby." The lawyer asked her about the art classes and decorating classes she attended. Next, he asked her to list the awards she received for the best-decorated houses. He questioned Sally about the teaching position she was offered at a community college. Sally embellished upon all her skills. In the end, Sally proved the case that she was truly talented and could go out and easily earn $75,000 a year—especially with the contacts she made—the wives of her husband's well-heeled business colleagues!

- *Make certain you are not going to court so you can finally have "your side of the story" heard. Court is not the place to vent your emotions. Save that for the therapist. Emotional gratification can often cost you dollars. Stay focused on your goal to get a good settlement.*

- *You need to be a good listener when you are the witness. Listen carefully to questions—paying special attention to how they are worded—and answer only what is asked. Never volunteer information. You should carefully review possible questions with your lawyer before you step foot into court.*

- *If you don't understand a question, say so. If you need clarification, ask for it.*

- *Avoid emotionality. Stay focused, serious, and calm.*

- *Don't be rude or sarcastic. When you are in court, everything about you is on trial. Don't constantly make faces when answering questions or listening to your spouse's response.*

- *Don't lie. Your credibility is at issue. Be truthful at all times.*

- *Speak in a clear, well-modulated voice.*

- *Dress appropriately. It is always best to dress conservatively, but you should also dress to suit your case. If you are making the statement that your lifestyle is expensive to maintain, feel free to wear your expensive jewelry and designer suits. If you are complaining that you are destitute, dress accordingly.*

- *Always be on time.*

- *Understand your case.*

- *Know your judge.*

KNOW YOUR JUDGE

A good lawyer will know all the judges sitting in the family court. It is essential that your lawyer knows how a judge habitually rules on certain issues. For example, if you are going before a judge or a master on the issue of earning capacity, your lawyer should know how that person has ruled on this issue in other cases. If your lawyer has not appeared before a particular judge before, he or she should be able to contact colleagues to gather information. It is also possible to get copies of a judge's published opinions. In addition, judges often lecture at colleges, universities, law schools, and continuing legal education classes and may have spoken on the issue relevant to your case. It is very important that you know a judge's biases. Knowing a judge's prior ruling history may change the way you see and plead your case. Let's suppose you're planning to argue that no earning capacity should be imputed to you. That tune could change if you learn that your judge believes that both parents should work as soon as children are in school.

Another important factor: Judges have varying levels of sophistication when it comes to understanding financial issues. If you have a case that is complicated financially, you may want to get your lawyer's advice as to whether or not your judge dealt knowledgeably with issues like those in your case in the past.

It is important to go into your case being fully prepared. You should consider all the variables and options that a judge may take into consideration before you set foot into a courtroom. Most cases generally end up settling at some point, but you may find that you need to be aggressive at some points in the process and go to court. Court is a last alternative; however, you may find that some issues can't be solved without at least the threat of a fight. Sometimes, faced with litigation, parties will decide it is wisest to settle. Your lawyer should help you decide the best course of action.

Chapter Fourteen

WHAT DOES A GOOD PROPERTY SETTLEMENT CONTAIN?

You can negotiate and get the greatest settlement in the world. However, if you don't have a properly worded agreement that contains the right clauses or the necessary language to enable you to get the property you bargained for and enforce that settlement, that settlement is not worth the paper it is written on. It is your lawyer's job to draft an agreement artfully, but for *you*, it is essential to know what should be in a good agreement.

Every property settlement agreement contains certain "boilerplate" clauses that are standard in property agreements. Remember, however, that your case is unique, so there will be certain clauses tailored to your needs.

Boilerplate economic clauses might include the following:

- *Background, including:*

  1. Any relevant identifying data

  2. Names of parties

  3. Residences

  4. Date of marriage and separation, if applicable

- *Names of parties' lawyers or statement that one or both parties represented themselves.*

- *Date of signing and any dates on which transactions may occur or property will be distributed.*

- *List of personal property and how it is to be split (example: household furnishings, carpets, jewelry, books, pictures, and other tangible personal property).*

- *Real estate: A list of all real estate and how the properties are to be split (example: marital home, vacation home, investment properties). List the following:*

  1. Who will pay all the expenses

  2. When the responsibility for such payment will begin

  3. Who will own the property or will it be sold; if it is to be sold, how the proceeds will be split

- *Full financial disclosure. This clause will list all assets and liabilities. Sometimes lawyers state that both parties are aware of the others' property and liabilities and waive a listing of the assets and debts. If you later discover that your spouse hid assets or failed to disclose any assets, you could overturn the property settlement agreement on the basis of fraud. So never waive this disclosure without checking with a lawyer!*

- *Retirement accounts and/or pension funds. List the following:*

1. *Who will keep the accounts*

2. *Whether a qualified domestic relations order needs to be written*

- *Disposition of all bank accounts. Detail who will take possession of every account.*

- *Disposition of all investments. Detail who will take possession of stocks, bonds, mutual funds, etc.*

- *Disposition of stock options. Detail how options will be split.*

- *Debts. Detail and specifically list who is responsible for which debts.*

- *Mutual general release. In this clause, both parties release the other from any and all debts owed now and in the future.*

- *Child support:*

  1. *Detail who will pay and the amount to be paid.*

  2. *Explain how it will be paid—through the courts or direct payment—and how long it will last.*

  3. *Specifically list what costs are covered.*

  4. *Detail whether one party will reimburse the other for expenses not covered in the agreement.*

  5. *Detail who will be responsible for special needs or extraordinary expenses.*

- *Health-care insurance and additional costs:*

  1. *Detail who is responsible for the cost.*

  2. *Detail how unreimbursed expenses will be treated.*

  3. *Specifically state who pays dental, orthodontic, and psychological expenses.*

- *Educational and extracurricular costs:*

  1. *Detail who is responsible to pay and for how long.*

  2. *You might want to address any unknown costs that may arise in the future.*

- *Alimony:*

  1. *Detail whether alimony or spousal support will be part of the settlement and for how long.*

  2. *Explain what form the support will take and the terms of the payment.*

- *Discuss the tax consequences of all transactions covered in the agreement including, but not limited to:*

  1. *Which parent shall take the dependency exemptions, head of household, and earned income credit.*

  2. *Who bears responsibility for capital gains, tax liabilities, and joint tax indemnification.*

- *Cars. Detail who gets which vehicles.*

- *Separate assets. Detail and list specifically how these will be divided.*

- *Bankruptcy provision. Detail what happens if one spouse declares bankruptcy.*

- *Disposition of any and all business interests. Detail who keeps the business and how the other spouse will be compensated.*

- *Enforcement provisions. State what happens if any provision of the agreement is not performed.*

- *Attorney's fees. State who will pay the costs.*

Please note this is not an exhaustive list. Your lawyer may want to add other clauses. The following are examples of more specific economic clauses that may be added to your agreement to protect your specific interests:

1. Life insurance to secure payment. *Let's say your agreement provides that you will receive spousal and child support for seven years. What happens if your ex dies after four years? Does your settlement make certain that you will get paid the amount you expected?*

   Your settlement should contain language that makes absolutely certain you will get the money if your ex dies. One way to guarantee that is to stipulate in your agreement that the supporting spouse purchase the necessary amount of life insurance, with you as the beneficiary, in the amount of the spousal and child support owed to you. That covers the support in the event of the supporting spouse's death—a wise precaution in many cases.

   Make certain that the name of the beneficiary on the insurance policy—or the person who will receive the money—is not changed at any time. The insurance company will pay the money only to the person named in the policy. Take all necessary steps to make sure that the beneficiary cannot be changed. Make certain you receive copies of all correspondence from the insurance company concerning this policy. Also stipulate that you will receive all correspondence between the supporting spouse and the insurance company. Stipulate, too, that the supporting spouse may make no changes in the policy without your written concurrence. If the supporting spouse already has a policy with someone else as the beneficiary but then it is agreed that you will become the new beneficiary, make certain that you receive a copy of the up-to-date policy with your name as the beneficiary. You cannot be too careful. You don't want to end up suing your ex's estate to collect your money.

2. Make certain the person who owns the policy doesn't borrow against it in excess of what is owed under the support obligation.

Many life insurance policies allow the owner of the policy to take out a loan against it. With many policies, if the owner dies while a loan is still outstanding against the policy, the policy's payout will be diminished by the amount outstanding. So in stipulating the policy, you will want to negotiate, first whether you or your ex will be the owner of the policy. Then, you want to make certain that your ex cannot borrow against the policy if it reduces the amount of the policy to less than the amount that you are owed for support. You can arrange for the recipient of the funds to own the policy until such time that the support obligation is fulfilled. Then you can arrange for the ownership to revert back to the obligor.

3. Make certain you know who is responsible for following through. *Someone is going to have to make certain that the premiums are paid and that your ex abides by all the provisions. So who will have that responsibility? You or your lawyer? Too often poor communication occurs between lawyer and client, and one thinks the other is taking care of business. Spell out clearly with your attorney whether you want to be the one to follow through on the policy or whether you would rather pay him or her to do so. Many lawyers will send out letters spelling out what their clients should do. Be certain to read all correspondence carefully so you know your role and what you need to do.*

Mike and Jane agree in their property settlement agreement that Mike will pay Jane $500 a month for five years—so that makes $6,000 a year for five years, or $30,000. To make certain Jane will get the money, Mike should be required to purchase a life insurance policy in the amount of $30,000 naming Jane as the irrevocable beneficiary. Mike should provide that he will send notice to Jane every time a premium is due and a separate notice that it has been paid.

In addition, Mike should agree that the insurance company will notify Jane if payments for the premiums have not been made. Mike should specifically authorize Jane to speak with the insurance company if she has any questions concerning payments, loan balances, and beneficiary designations, and provide a copy of a letter sent to the insurance company that permits this contact.

In addition, Mike can provide written instructions that Jane is the irrevocable beneficiary and that this designation of Jane as the beneficiary may not be changed until the insurance company receives proof that the obligation has been fully satisfied. Mike can provide that Jane shall remain the owner of the policy until such time as his spousal and child support obligation is paid off. It is very important to identify the name and the amount of the policy in the agreement. If there is any other important information, the kind of policy, the amount, the terms, or the identity and responsibilities of you and your spouse, that information should be included as well.

You should protect yourself in the same way if you are receiving alimony, spousal support, or any other financial obligation that remains outstanding under the property settlement agreement. For example, if you have any cash distributions or property distributions outstanding, you may want to buy life insurance to guarantee those payments, too.

Whether you are the person getting the support payments or the person paying, you will need to know your rights and responsibilities. Ask the following questions if you will be getting child or spousal support or alimony or any other property distribution as part of your settlement agreement:

- *Shouldn't my ex have to buy a life insurance policy to secure any support payments in case of death?*

- *How will I know for sure that the premiums have been paid?*

- *What guarantees will I have that I remain the beneficiary?*

- *Can I own the policy?*

- *If I own the policy while I am receiving payments, once the payments are completed, will the policy revert back to my ex?*

- *Will my ex be able to borrow against the policy? Can I prevent this from occurring?*

- *What happens if I remarry? Will it affect my right to remain a beneficiary?*

- *If my ex can't get life insurance, can I get a lien on any property that he or she owns?*

- *What other measure can I take to protect the money or property owed to me?*

- *Is insurance available through an employer or retirement plan?*

> *One option you may want to check into is limiting the amount of life insurance to the amount of the debt owed by purchasing a decreasing term policy. Check with your lawyer.*

4. Specify how joint debt will be split. *When divorcing, it is always best to try to take on only debt for which you are solely responsible. If you and your spouse have accumulated joint debt during the marriage, you are both responsible for paying it. For instance, if you are joint signatories—you are both cardholders—on a credit card, both of you are responsible for paying for the purchases made with that card, whether or not the given purchases were actually used by you. You may both want to consider borrowing money in your own names to pay off the joint debt and then being responsible only for the debt you have in your own name.*

One spouse will often take on the responsibility of paying a joint debt. Let's say, the wife moves out of the marital home. The husband remains in the home and agrees to pay the mortgage.

Both the husband's and wife's name remain on the mortgage. (Taking her name off the mortgage would require refinancing, and the husband doesn't have the money to refinance, so his wife's name remains.) If the husband loses his job after six months and defaults on the mortgage, the mortgage company can go after the wife to pay the mortgage.

The wife takes out the property settlement agreement and reads the statement that her husband agrees to "hold harmless and indemnify wife" against any liability she may owe on the mortgage. This clause is legalese for the proposition that the husband agreed to pay the mortgage and won't ask his wife for the money. The problem is that the mortgage company is a third party and is not bound by the property settlement agreement. The mortgage, on the other hand, is a contract among the husband, the wife, and the financial institution. You should note, however, that it is always better to have a "hold harmless" clause in your agreement. You may be in a better position to argue that you are not liable for the mortgage payments than without this clause.

This situation illustrates that even in the best-worded property agreements, you still may have problems when you and your ex remain liable for a joint debt after you divorce. If at all possible, word your settlement agreement so that (a) your debt responsibility is specifically detailed and spelled out, and (b) you are responsible for only your share of the debt. Preferably, limit your payment of the debt to only that debt which is in your name alone.

From a transactional viewpoint, depending on the terms of your settlement, you may want to consider whether or not it would be better to sell the house to avoid any future liability. Another option that may work is to ask your spouse to find a family member who might be willing to co-sign for the mortgage. Always consider the pros and cons of each transaction.

5. Determine what will happen in the event of bankruptcy. *Bank-ruptcy happens—especially when divorce enters the picture. When it happens in the presence of divorce, it can raise many issues. You may want to consider that child and spousal support as well as al-imony payments are not discharged in a bankruptcy proceeding. That means you cannot get rid of your obligation to pay these pay-ments by filing for bankruptcy. If you have any inkling that your ex might be contemplating bankruptcy, or if your soon-to-be-ex has a great deal of debt, you will want to be specific in the wording of an agreement. Any payments in your agreement that are character-ized as property distribution may be discharged in bankruptcy. Suppose you accept a 50 percent property split, but you have to wait three years to get most of the money. If your ex files for bank-ruptcy, he or she could discharge that obligation. If, however, you were to opt to take that amount of money as alimony payments, that obligation could not be discharged in bankruptcy. If your ex files for bankruptcy, he or she will still be responsible for making alimony payments, as alimony payments are not dischargeable in bankruptcy. You are not expected to know the legalese in an agree-ment, but you certainly can ask your lawyer if you are protected if your ex files bankruptcy.*

Bankruptcy can also be a problem when splitting your debt. Jeff and Susan didn't earn a lot of money during their marriage. However, they both used their joint credit cards frequently. The credit cards were in both names, and the contract with the card company obligated both Susan and Jeff to pay the debts. By the time they separated, they each had spent more than $50,000 on the cards. When they divorced, Jeff agreed to assume responsibil-ity for half that amount, which amounted to assuming the pay-ments for three of their joint credit cards. Susan assumed the responsibility for two other cards. Susan borrowed money from her parents and paid off the credit cards within three months. Jeff,

*however, filed for bankruptcy nine months after the divorce. Susan
didn't know that Jeff had filed for bankruptcy or that he'd had all
his credit card debt discharged in the bankruptcy. Jeff was no
longer responsible to pay that portion of the debt. The credit card
company then went after Susan to pay the debt. Because Susan
was jointly responsible for the debt, she had to pay.*

The credit card company is not bound by your settlement
agreement, because they are not a party to the agreement, but it is
always better to make it clear in your property agreement what
debts each party is responsible for. It is always better not to have
outstanding debt in joint names after a divorce. Sometimes it can't
be avoided, and if you are in this situation and your ex-spouse files
for bankruptcy, you are allowed to petition the bankruptcy court to
except the joint debt from the bankruptcy. (This means you are asking the court to take the specific debt out of the bankruptcy proceedings so the person filing for bankruptcy—in this case your
ex—will still be responsible for paying the debt.) Of course, if you
don't know that your ex is filing for bankruptcy, you will not be
able to object and request that the debt not be wiped out. You may
want to provide a clause in your property settlement agreement
that either party has to notify the other within twenty-fours hours if
they file bankruptcy at any time before paying off joint debts, even
if the filing is after the divorce.

You may also want to include language in the property settlement agreement that characterizes the payment of the joint marital
debt as alimony or child support. (Child support and spousal support or alimony are not dischargeable in bankruptcy.) True, the
bankruptcy court is not bound by this language, and a judge can
still decide that the payment is not support and can discharge the
debt. However, you should do everything in your power to make
certain that you do not get stuck paying for debt that your ex
agreed to pay.

In sum, it is best not to have outstanding joint debt after divorce *if you can avoid it. Ask your lawyer the best way to protect you from this situation. You will want to spell out in your agreement exactly which debts each of you is assuming.*

> ▪ *Be certain to ask your lawyer if any of the provisions in your property settlement agreement could be adversely affected in any bankruptcy proceeding.*

6. Make certain you get what you agreed to. *There are other important clauses about which you might want to inquire. You will need language in your agreement that allows you to sue in court and enforce the agreement. It is your lawyer's job to put in the proper language, but ask questions to make certain you will be able to sue in court to enforce any provisions of the agreement that the other party has not completed.*

7. Find out if you need to file a copy of your property settlement agreement along with the divorce decree. *You may also want to ask your lawyer if your state requires you to file a copy of the property settlement agreement along with your divorce decree. Some lawyers prefer not to attach a copy, if possible, because if your state permits anyone to get a copy of your file and review your settlement, you may find other interested persons going down to the court to check on your settlement. Worse yet, you may find your future dates checking out the property you got in your divorce to see if you have assets. Ask your lawyer if you can do anything to prevent the public from looking into your divorce settlement.*

8. Protect yourself if you discover after the divorce that your ex has more assets than revealed before the divorce. *When you negotiate your settlement, you agree to split the property based on your*

knowledge of what property is in the marital pot. Generally, clauses are written into such agreements disclosing that both you and your spouse know what assets the other has. Some lawyers will even attach a list of all the assets as an exhibit. Often, however, there is just a clause that each spouse knows what assets the other spouse owns under the agreement and that each agrees to give up all right to any of those assets once the settlement takes effect. If you think your spouse has any assets of which you are not aware, you may want to ask your lawyer if you can include language in the agreement that any assets not listed in the agreement (and in this case you may want to include a list of all the assets each party claims to own) may be subject to distribution even after the divorce proceedings have ended. This could come in handy if, soon after the divorce, your ex buys a new vacation home, new car, and boat, yet claimed in your agreement the only marital asset was the house! Seems your ex had more than he or she claimed. Agreements can be overturned if it was based on fraud or misrepresentation. Check with your lawyer to make certain that everything that can possibly be done to protect you will be done.

9. Protect yourself if you have filed joint tax returns and are concerned your spouse might not have been honest. If you and your spouse have always filed joint tax returns, you may want to include a provision in your agreement providing that if it is later discovered that any back taxes, interest, and penalties are due, the party responsible for the mistake in the calculations will be responsible for paying the tax. If you and your spouse file a joint tax return, then both parties are liable for any taxes later found to be due. However, you may want to ask your lawyer about adding a clause that the party who is responsible for any mistakes will be held responsible to pay the tax.

10. Modify any general release clause. *Most divorce agreements contain a "general release clause," in which each spouse waives all right to file any future claims against the other spouse for any reason. Make certain that you waive only known claims. You never know what bizarre secrets time will reveal. Today, with sexually transmitted diseases, an ex-spouse may discover an extramarital disease after the divorce. If you find yourself in that position and you can prove you got an STD from your ex, you don't want to preclude yourself from being able to file a tort claim—a claim for money damages—later on.*

11. You may want to make a distinction between receiving property as spousal support or part of property distribution. *How can I prevent my spouse from double dipping or getting credit twice for the same piece of property? Sometimes, if you're not careful, your spouse can "double dip"—that is, get a share of your assets in the property division and, should you later sell any of those assets, try to get the money from that sale classified as income or money available for any existing support obligations.*

    While going through the divorce process, you may be too emotional to care how the "money" you receive is labeled. However, this attitude can cost you in the end. In addition to the difference in tax considerations between payments that are considered to be alimony and payments that are considered to be equitable distribution, there are other considerations. You may want to clearly define in the property agreement what should happen if you are in this position.

    Sam and Marie split after twelve years of marriage. Both worked in a business together. In their divorce negotiations, it was agreed that Sam would pay Marie a lump-sum amount of money for her share of the business. A clause in the agreement provided that Marie could ask for an increase in alimony if

Sam's income later increased. In addition, Marie received alimony for seven years. The alimony was not part of the sale of the business. Three years after the divorce, Sam decided to sell the business. Marie went back to court to ask for an increase in alimony, stating that Sam had more money available to pay for alimony because he received a large sum of money for his business.

Sam could have placed a clause in the agreement stating that he paid Marie for her share of the business, and should the business be sold while his alimony obligation is still outstanding, the money received from the sale should not be considered income for alimony purposes. True, he sold the business while he was still paying alimony, and received money from the sale. But Marie has already received her share of the business during the property division. If allowed, this, in essence, would be giving Marie two bites at the apple—she would be getting a lump-sum amount for her share of the business and then get more money in alimony from the business. If you take the money Sam gets from the business and consider it as extra income available for alimony payments, you would count that money twice and Marie would be "double dipping." These double dip questions in which a spouse tries to take advantage of the same sum of money more than once, can occur in other instances.

The double dip question also is important if you or your spouse owns a business with retained earnings (money that is kept in a business). Should you try to go after retained earnings as income for alimony purposes or wait and try for a higher percentage of the money from his business in equitable distribution? The question is one of valuation. Should you consider the retained earnings as part of the business valuation for property distribution, or should you consider the retained earnings as money available for support purposes? If your spouse owns a business, *check with your lawyer to review this issue. (Refer to Chapter Seven on valuation of a business.)*

12. Consider the tax consequences. *Every property settlement must take tax consequences into consideration. Not every piece of property is equal to another. A house worth $650,000 is not equal to $650,000 in cash. When you sell a home, there are certain tax consequences. If you take stock as part of your settlement, there will be tax consequences when you sell the stock. You need to get advice from a financial or tax consultant when negotiating your property settlement.*

 You will also need to consider income tax consequences: tax credits, tax deductions, and filing status. For example, if you are the primary custodian of the children, you will be entitled to the favorable head of household tax credit unless you negotiate otherwise. You may also be entitled to tax credit for child care, depending on your income. Get advice from an accountant or other financial expert to figure out how best to split your tax credits and deductions. One party may use tax consequences to his or her benefit, while the other party chooses to get more cash. Find out what is best for you.

 In any property negotiation, the crucial thing is to make certain that the amount of money you bargain for is the amount you will receive and that it doesn't shrink because of tax consequences either now or in the future.

13. Include a clause that states that both spouses agree to sign all forms necessary to effectuate the agreement. *You will find yourself signing a great many forms, and you may never have heard of nor understand all of them. Get the advice of a lawyer or relevant expert. Many times different forms will need to be signed, and you may not be aware of all of them. And it is always best to*

include a clause that states that both parties agree to sign whatever forms necessary to effectuate the property settlement agreement. If you don't, you might find yourself back in court trying to
get your ex to sign forms received after your divorce. For example, some forms for change in beneficiary of some retirement
plans cannot, by law, be signed until after you are divorced. If a
pension requires that you sign a change in beneficiary form after
your divorce rather than before it could be trouble, because,
once the divorce has been concluded, your spouse may claim he
or she has no further duties and may refuse to change the beneficiary. So here again, add language to the property settlement
agreement that both spouses agree to sign all the necessary
papers to effectuate the agreement. Your lawyers may also ask
both spouses to sign the change-in-beneficiary forms when the
property settlement agreement is signed and then hold on to the
forms and submit them to the pension company after the divorce
is final.

Forms you may have to sign after a divorce may include the following:

- Quitclaim deed

- Refinancing documents

- Car titles

- Change-in-beneficiary forms

- Qualified Domestic Relations Order

BE PRECISE

The words used to draft your agreement should be clear and specific. One beauty of the law is that it can be very precise. But one person's precision can be another's confusion. That's why you need to go over every aspect of your divorce papers with your lawyer. Ask your lawyer to go over all the issues in your case. Make certain that there are clauses in your agreement that dispose of all the issues in your case.

Chapter Fifteen

YOUR WORST NIGHTMARES

Judges, lawyers, financial advisers, and clients have told war stories over the years about various divorce nightmares. The following are recurring patterns, some frequently asked questions, and tips on what to watch out for so you don't look back and say, "If I only knew . . ." Regard this chapter as a list of things you want to avoid.

EVERY LAWYER'S, JUDGE'S, PARENT'S, AND DIVORCE CLIENT'S NIGHTMARE

Nightmare #1: Failure to Document

John and Tracey marry. They move into an apartment for a few years. When Tracey finds out she is pregnant, they begin house hunting. Right after the birth of their first child, they find a great starter home in a neighborhood with young families. Tracey plans on quitting work and staying home with her child. John doesn't earn a great deal of money, but Tracey's parents are well off, and Tracey is used to asking them for financial help.

Tracey's dad, Bob, offered to give Tracey $20,000 for a down payment on their $60,000 home. Tracey gratefully accepts the money. Bob loves helping his little girl. Two years later, Tracey and John have another child. Tracey announces that she wants to redecorate the family room and the kitchen. Bob wants Tracey to be happy, so he finances the renovations to the tune of $25,000.

Ten years later, there's trouble in paradise. John announces he wants out of the marriage. He moves into his parents' home and files for divorce. John wants Tracey to sell the house. He wants half the proceeds. (They have no other assets.) Tracey doesn't want to disrupt the children. She asks her father to buy out John's half of the house. Bob is furious. The house is now worth $120,000. John told Bob he wanted $50,000 to get out of the marriage. Bob told him to pound sand. He stated, "I loaned you $45,000 to get the house and fix it up. I don't owe you anything. I financed your comfortable lifestyle for ten years now."

The problem: Now that the marriage is over, Bob says the money was not a gift, but a loan. However, Bob has no document—for example, a note or mortgage or any other written documentation—to prove that the money he gave Tracey was a loan and not a gift to the marriage. Because Bob is not able to substantiate the money was, indeed, a loan, he may not be able to get any back. If Tracey wants the house, she will have to buy out John's marital portion.

A judge from the Midwest told me of this same nightmare that grieves her not only as a judge but also as a parent. In the nightmare, she loans one of her children money for a down payment to buy a house. She never takes any legal steps to prove that the money is a loan and not a gift. No one likes to be legalistic about marriage or family matters. The judge is no exception. However, she knows the law of property division. The judge is fully aware that she needs to document the loan—if, indeed, the transaction is to be characterized as a loan in the event of a divorce.

Once the money is put into a joint asset—in this case the purchase of a marital home in both the child's name and the spouse's name—the asset becomes joint marital property subject to division at the time of divorce. The child may not get credit for money placed into a joint asset. Neither the child nor the parent is guaranteed reimbursement of all the money. The parent or child may be able to argue that some credit should be given for a part, if not all the money; however, without loan documentation, it may be lost. Remember, you marry for love, but divorce is all about money.

If you or another family member puts any substantial sum of money into joint marital property and expects it back if your marriage fails, you need to take the necessary steps to protect the money when it is given.

One family lawyer from the Midwest gives this good advice: There is nothing wrong with giving money to your kids—even a substantial sum—by way of a loan. It becomes a debt against both your child and his or her spouse and in the event of divorce, and you can claim the money you are owed. If you want to loan them the money for a down payment on a house, document it. That way, whether they stay married or divorce, you'll have a clear right to the money. By the same token, the lawyer recommends that if you give money to your child and not to the marriage, you also need to specify that it's being given as a gift only to your child, either by writing a letter that the money is only for your child, or by filling out forms or documents that might be necessary. He recommends filing a gift tax form, if necessary. If you give a gift of money and want that to remain separate property, you should have your child segregate the funds and keep them in a separate account, not the joint account.

It may pay to consult a lawyer in your state to help you decide what risks you are willing to take with the money. If you don't care if you or your child do not get "credit" for the money should a divorce occur—in other words, if you're willing to risk it—you may not need to do anything to document the transaction. If you do care, and especially if the marriage seems to be in trouble, you need to take precautions. You may even be able to structure a loan in which there are minimal repayments in the short run with larger sums of money being repaid in ten years. If you decide to forgive the loan later, you may be able to do so. Check with an accountant or other expert to structure your loan properly. (If you are contemplating divorce and you find yourself in this position, you may want to check with a lawyer to see if there is anything you can do now to rectify this situation.)

A VIEW FROM THE BENCH

A judge from the Northeast gives this sage advice: Document, document, document. Keep any separate money separate. That is, if you want to give money to one spouse, document that the money is solely for one spouse. If you have not done this, you should at the very least have documentation for all amounts given or spent and show how, why, and to whom. If you get gifts or loans, get copies of the estate tax returns and/or the gift tax returns that indicate how and where you received the money. Then, secure the receipts or other documentation that shows where and how you spent the money. You may have to make telephone calls to get this documentation, but it may be time well spent. You can argue in a divorce settlement that you should be given credit for those gifts and other expenditures as your contribution to the marriage.

Nightmare #2: Not Keeping Separate Property Separate

Sam and Helen, both professors, met shortly after Sam's divorce from his first wife. After a short courtship, they married. Sam owned the house they were living in, and they wanted a fresh start. So Sam sold the house, took all the money from the sale, and rolled the proceeds (all $200,000) into a new home that Sam and Helen owned jointly. Their new home cost $450,000, so they both assumed responsibility for the mortgage of $250,000. Sam probably should have struck a legal agreement with Helen that the $200,000 was his money, and so that if they were to divorce, Sam would get credit for the first $200,000 paid into their house. But he didn't. Seven years into the marriage, Sam realized that the marriage wasn't working and divorce was the only answer. In the meantime, the house needed a new roof and there was a great deal of water damage and structural damage that had occurred. The housing market had not appreciated, and the house by this time needed about $150,000 of work before it could be sold.

Sam wanted to keep the house. He figured he would spend time making the repairs. After all, he put *his* $200,000 into the house. Right? Not necessarily. Check out the law in your state. You may be faced with the situation that once you take separate property—$200,000 from the sale of Sam's first home—and put it into property owned jointly with a new spouse, it becomes marital property. Helen earned half of what Sam earned, and she believed that she should be paid for her half of the house—meaning fully half of the house's total value. She felt that the full $200,000 belonged to both of them. In addition, she wanted no part of the cost of repairs. She was angry and wanted to get as much of Sam's pension as she possibly could. Sam could not believe that he would have to give Helen anything. He felt it was "morally wrong" that Helen would not acknowledge that *his* money had bought the house.

Get over two notions: (1) that moral right and wrong should govern property distribution and (2) the idea that divorce is fair! As it turned out, Sam and Helen compromised out of court, but Sam came close to losing much of what he believed was his rightful money. He learned the hard way that if he wants to keep his property separate, he has to take the legal steps to do so.

Nightmare #3: Spouse Using Credit Card to Hide Money

One forensic accountant suggests that when looking for hidden assets, look at credit card transactions. One time-honored trick is to make large overpayments to the credit company. For instance, if your spouse owes $1,500 on a credit card, he or she can make a payment of $3,000. The extra money in effect becomes a bank account. Let's say you have ten cards with a few thousand dollars or more overpaid on each. You can end up hiding a considerable amount of money. In addition, you can withdraw money on a card and make the transaction appear as payments on the statement. In one case, the wife "borrowed" a few thousand dollars each month on different cards.

Another way of sinking money into a card is to apply for a secured credit card. With such a secured credit card, you send in a deposit to ensure your credit and then you borrow against that deposit. In one case, a spouse applied for a secured credit card and, in order to guarantee a $10,000 limit, she took the ten grand from the couple's savings account.

Credit cards can invite other dangers. It is a well-known tactic for one partner, angry over impending divorce, to go on a spending spree, maxing out credit cards held jointly with the spouse. True, this will anger the spouse—but it could also bring on bankruptcy.

Destroying joint credit cards during separation may seem wise on the surface, but think again. A lawyer from the Midwest states that she knows judges who have looked unfavorably on spouses who, by destroying credit cards, left their partner without the ability to buy clothing or groceries for their kids. This lawyer's advice is that before cutting off credit cards, have proof that your spouse spends extravagantly. Yes, there is risk involved. You may end up being liable for large debts if you make an error in judgment. So consider what you know about your spouse. If you think he or she may run up incredible bills, you may want to take your chances with judges who may disapprove and cancel the cards. If you do this, make certain that you pay for the necessities. Otherwise, your spouse can claim in court that you have been negligent.

One lawyer from the Southwest recounted a story of a wife who had her new boyfriend call the credit card company to extend the credit limit on an existing card. After the wife ran up an incredible bill, the husband realized what happened. The wife later declared bankruptcy. This lawyer recommends that it may be wise, if your spouse is a spendthrift, to consider canceling all joint credit cards and making certain that you give your spouse enough money to pay the bills. Check with an attorney.

After divorce, you must write a letter to the credit card company informing them that you are divorced. Ideally, you will close any joint accounts and cut up any cards. If the card company refuses to close the account, specify clearly in your letter that you will not be responsible for any charges your ex or soon-to-be-ex makes. (The credit card company may still try to go after you for charges. You stand a better chance, however, of making a winning argument if you document in writing that you shall bear no further responsibility.)

Nightmare #4: Hiding Money in Insurance Policies

Any institution in the business of accepting money will accept money any time, even in advance. You can prepay or overpay on insurance annuities or other annuities. One forensic accountant recommends that you check all payments very carefully.

Nightmare #5: Stashing Cash

People stash cash wherever they think they can get away with it. One accountant tells the story of someone buying land for cash and neglecting to record the deed to the real estate. One lawyer tells of a client who opened custodial accounts for their children and started depositing large sums of money into the accounts a year before separation. (If you do choose to give money to a child and put it into a Uniform Gift to Minors Account [UGMA], you may find that you cannot use the money or get it back if you divorce. Your spouse may contest the use of any money spent that does not benefit your child.)

Another story involves a criminal lawyer going through his own divorce who deposited large retainers in an attorney trust account and claimed the money was not his when, in fact, he had already tried the case and had earned his fee. Another transaction involves the generous soul who lends money to someone interest-free during divorce proceedings. Transactions like these may include money that should more properly be added back into the marital estate.

For tax purposes, business owners often claim their personal expenses as business expenses and take them as tax deductions. Another trick to watch out for is the padding of payroll taxes. Deductions for payroll taxes need to be reasonable in relationship to the payroll. If you find 40 to 50 percent being deducted in taxes, you better look for the refund coming back.

"It's easy to hide money if you own a business," recounts one financial planner. Look for the girlfriend on the payroll or the business owner taking a significant other on a "business trip" to the Bahamas. And don't just limit your search of phantom employees to girlfriends. Check to see if relatives or friends of your spouse are on the payroll. You may find a number of "new" employees who have surfaced since the divorce planning began. When an employee starts padding the payroll with phantom employees, the money claimed but not really paid to anyone, often magically reappears in the employer's possession after the divorce.

You may need an expert to help you look into a business's inventory. Inventories are good places to hide cash or property. One accountant tells of a business owner who claimed that all his inventory had ended up on a truck and had absolutely no value. The truck was located and examined, but all the "worthless inventory" was about to be transferred to a buyer willing to pay a lot of money for it. Another accountant tells of a business owner who sent inventory to a buyer who agreed to house it for "safe keeping" until after the divorce, when it would be returned for sale. You may need a business valuator to analyze the company's sales patterns. Money can and often does get lost when divorce rears its ugly head.

If your spouse owns a business, you might want to get copies of all checks written by the business. Some checks might be to relatives or friends who might have volunteered to "hold" some money for your spouse until after the divorce. Also look for checks made out to cash. If you find more than a few checks written to cash for significant amounts, you might want to get the original canceled checks and look on the back to see where the checks were deposited. You may find that you can uncover some new bank accounts.

One accountant from the Southwest did an audit on a business whose owner had turned off the audit feature on his computer software program and deleted transactions. The owner used a software program that enabled him to delete every transaction periodically. When the computer system crashed, he couldn't restore the information, and he tried to change data. When he was questioned by a forensic accountant about his inventory, he couldn't answer questions and got very nervous, and his scheme unraveled.

This wise accountant recommends using the Internal Revenue Service guidelines for the indices of fraud if you suspect your spouse is lying or hiding money. These guidelines are as follows:

1. Refusals to answer questions

2. Hostile demeanor when asking pertinent questions

3. Consistent delay in providing information

4. Answering questions in a threatening manner

In one case, a lawyer represented a husband who was in business with his wife. The couple used joint credit cards to fund the business, as well as one joint checking account. The husband trusted his wife not to fool around with the money that ran the business that fed and clothed them. One day he went to make a withdrawal and discovered that his wife had taken all the money out of their joint account. The husband went to court to get the money back. Because the business funds and the personal finances were intermingled, however, the judge ruled that the money removed from the account would be dealt with later in equitable distribution. When in business with a spouse, take the necessary business precautions to protect the assets!

Nightmare #6: Hidden Assets

Many people believe that their spouses are hiding money. Maybe they are. But it's also true that lawyers may spend a great deal of money on discovery, trying to find hidden assets, and you end up with only a large legal bill. If you believe your spouse is hiding money, you may want to consult with a forensic account-ant. One way to figure out whether your spouse is playing around with numbers is to do an itemization of income and expense.

One method you can use is a cost-of-living analysis. For exam-ple, if your spouse is in a cash business and claims on his tax return that his or her yearly income is $15,000, you might want to figure out what assets he or she owns and also how much is spent each month. Especially when dealing with businesses in which only cash is accepted or payment is largely received in cash, you may find that the amount of income reported to the federal govern-ment is grossly under-reported. If you find this is the case, you must seek the advice of a lawyer to determine how best to deal with the support and property division issues. If a spouse has under-reported income—especially if you jointly signed the tax return—you and your spouse may be open together to liability for tax evasion.

Is it wise to spend a lot of money to find out where the money is? Just how much money you want to spend to determine whether your spouse is hiding income and assets? One judge states that you should look before you leap:

A husband and wife both accused the other of lying and cheat-ing and were insistent that their lawyers find the hidden money. They both wanted "their fair share" and were determined to find out how much they each deserved. The parties paid their lawyers a small fortune to pursue discovery to uncover where the money was hidden. Both husband and wife owed significant amounts of money in back taxes and had maxed out their credit cards—and both had quite a few. They had always lived beyond their means. They spent all the money they had and also money they bor-rowed. They did not uncover any money—just debt. The hus-band and wife ended up with large legal bills and no money. Had either used a financial expert to review all the financial information in the beginning, each may have saved money later spent on legal fees. But sometimes couples review the numbers and anger prevents them from believing what they see. Remember: It's *your* money you stand to lose.

When you suspect that your spouse is hiding money, you may want to determine a ballpark amount you are willing to spend on finding out. One aggrieved spouse was convinced her partner was hiding money from a cash business. Many lawyers advised that it would be too difficult to find it. One lawyer was willing to look for the cash as long as the spouse realized that the hunt could get expensive. Thousands of dollars and significant time spent by forensic accountants uncovered significant additional assets and income.

So remember: These things take time and money. Before starting such a search, pick a dollar amount over which you are not willing to go. Give forensic accountants and private investigators a budget that they must not exceed. Review the findings with your lawyer along the way to determine whether the money spent has yielded results that warrant spending more money.

Nightmare #7: Offshore Accounts

People have been known to stash cash in offshore accounts in the Bahamas, Indonesia, Ireland, Switzerland, the Seychelles, and elsewhere. You need expert help if you suspect your spouse has hidden money offshore. Foreign countries won't allow fishing expeditions, and you will need to know what questions to ask. Check with a lawyer.

Nightmare #8: Common Mistakes

When questioning lawyers and judges about mistakes their clients made, the following were placed in the "too dumb to be believed" category, although one judge remarks, "We are all fools in love":

- *Man and woman marry. The husband owes $30,000 to an ex-wife for a lump-sum payment in equitable distribution. The husband and new wife mortgage their home, which they own jointly, to pay off the debt to his first wife. Two years later, the husband and new wife divorce. But the $30,000 isn't paid off yet. She has to share the cost of paying off his marital debt from his first marriage. The moral of this story: Don't agree to use joint marital property to pay for debts to former spouses.*

- *Man and woman marry. The wife takes the home she received in settlement from a previous divorce and puts her and her new husband's name on the deed. The wife had given up any rights to her first husband's pension to keep the house. Five years later, the wife and new husband divorce. The wife has to split the house with husband #2. This shows how differently we feel about cash vs. real estate. Had the wife taken part of her first husband's pension plan as part of first divorce settlement, she would never have handed over part of that pension to her second husband. It would have seemed rightfully her property. But with a house, we often feel very differently. Now the wife is struggling to keep a roof over her head. Moral: Don't be sentimental about real estate. Keep your personal, separate property personal and separate.*

- *Man and woman marry. Ten years into the marriage, both are unhappy. Six months before the wife leaves, the husband inherits a beach house that has been in his family for many years. The husband thinks he will make wife happy by putting both names on the beach house deed. Six months later, he finds out that he has to fork over a great deal of money to his wife when they split so he can keep the beach house in the family. One family law court administrator commented on this case: "No good deed goes unpunished." If you must give away something, realize that in many states the appreciation of property—the amount the property rises in value from* the time it was received until the time you separate—may be included as part of the marital property. Your spouse will share in something. If you are having an unhappy marriage and you want to make your spouse happy, go to a psychologist or counselor for advice. But it's probably not the wisest idea in the world to use property to make a disgruntled spouse happy.

POSTSCRIPT

Divorce is a life-altering event. It changes your life, but it does not have to destroy it. During the process of divorce, use your time wisely. Take an inventory of your life. Don't forget to make a list of all the things in your life you should be thankful for!

- *Get whatever help you need to get over your anger and work through your emotions.*

- *Focus on the money.*

- *Collect all the financial data necessary to secure your financial future.*

- *Interview prospective experts who can help you.*

- *Decide what you need to go forward with your life.*

- *Determine the route you need to take to get your divorce.*

- *Cut your best business deal.*

- *Move on with the rest of your life.*

You can take charge of the process and take control of your life. What route you take needn't be dictated by a third party. It may not appear so now, but looking back you will be surprised at just how much you have learned. Some clients have confided in me that they feel as if they truly learned from this process and came out of it stronger and more emotionally balanced.

GLOSSARY

ACTUARY: A person trained in valuing pensions and determining their worth. An actuary can also compute insurance premium rates, risks, and other data based on a statistical analysis.

AFFIDAVIT: A sworn statement of facts.

ALIMONY: Monetary payments made by one spouse to another for support of that spouse following divorce. The number of years a person receives such payments is usually determined by a fact-finder. Other terms for this payment may include spousal support and maintenance.

ALLEGATION: A claim by one party against another.

ALTERNATE PAYEE: The person, generally the nonemployed spouse, who receives certain benefits under a pension plan.

ANNUITY: An investment contract between you and an insurance company for a specified period of time.

ANSWER: A written response to a complaint or petition.

APPRAISAL: Valuing or determining the worth of an asset.

ARBITRATION: A dispute-resolution process in which both spouses go before one person who listens to both sides of the case. The arbitrator then makes a decision in the case.

ASSETS: All property owned by either spouse that has a monetary value.

BENEFICIARY: A person who is designated to receive certain benefits or money.

BUSINESS VALUATOR: A person trained to analyze the books and records of a business and determine its worth.

CHAMBERS: A room generally right next to the courtroom. A judge might hold conferences with lawyers or interview small children in chambers.

COBRA (CONSOLIDATED OMNIBUS BUDGET RECONCILIATION ACT OF 1985): This federal law enables a spouse to continue health-care coverage under an existing policy for up to thirty-six months following a divorce.

COLLABORATIVE LAW: An alternative dispute process in which both parties and their counsel pledge to resolve the case without going to trial.

COMMUNITY PROPERTY: Property acquired by both spouses during a marriage, exclusive of gifts or inheritance.

COMPLAINT: A written pleading or document that begins the divorce process. The complaint sets forth the facts and requests specific relief.

CONSUMER CREDIT COUNSELOR: A person who can review your monthly budget, provide advice on the use of credit cards, helps consolidate debts, and sometimes helps with budgeting and assisting you with questions about credit.

CPA (CERTIFIED PUBLIC ACCOUNTANT): A CPA can help you with basic tax questions.

CROSS-EXAMINATION: The questioning of a witness by the opposing party at a trial or deposition.

DECREE: The final ruling in a case.

DEFENDANT: The party against whom a legal action is filed.

DEFINED BENEFIT PLAN: A pension plan in which an employer promises to pay a fixed or certain benefit to an employee upon retirement. The amount may be determined by a formula. Employees do not contribute to this plan.

DEFINED CONTRIBUTION PLAN: A retirement plan in which a certain sum of money is set aside every year by the employer for the employee. Employers and employees may contribute to this type of retirement plan. The amount the employees will receive may fluctuate depending on the investment.

DEPOSITION: The testimony of a witness taken out of court. It is sometimes referred to as a mini-hearing in which the witness answers questions under oath. A deposition is generally taken during the discovery process.

DIRECT EXAMINATION: The initial questioning of a witness by the lawyer who calls that witness to the stand.

DISCOVERY: The formal proceedings in which both parties to a legal action seek to find out information from the opposing side. This process takes place prior to a formal hearing. In divorce, counsel may file interrogatories or written questions or take a deposition or a mini-hearing to determine the size and contents of the marital estate.

EMANCIPATION: The age at which a child is no longer considered a minor.

EQUITABLE DISTRIBUTION: The method used by the majority of states to divide property which takes into account approximately eleven factors to reach a "fair" split.

ERISA (EMPLOYEE RETIREMENT INCOME SECURITY ACT): This federal law sets certain minimum standards for pension plans provided by employers in private industry.

FACT-FINDER: Any of a number of people, including hearing officers, masters, and judges, who listen to a case and decide the outcome of some of or all the issues.

FORENSIC ACCOUNTANT: An accountant trained to analyze tax returns and other financial information in order to determine the value of a business and other assets and decide whether one spouse may be hiding assets.

GARNISHMENT: A method of payment of child support whereby a spouse's employer deducts the child support payment from an employee's paycheck and sends it into the court. The court, in turn, mails out a check to the recipient of the child support order.

HOLD-HARMLESS: An agreement whereby one party assumes responsibility for a debt or obligation and further agrees to protect the other party from loss or expense based on that obligation.

INDEMNIFICATION: A promise to reimburse another person in the event of a loss.

INTERROGATORIES: Written questions sent by a lawyer to the other party that are answered under oath within a certain prescribed period of time.

JOINT PROPERTY: Property held in the name of more than one person.

JURISDICTION: The power vested in a court to decide certain issues.

LIABILITIES: Debts owed by either spouse.

MARITAL ESTATE: The assets or property and accumulated income acquired by spouses during marriage.

MEDIATION: A method of dispute resolution in which both spouses use the skill of a third person to help negotiate and reach a settlement on some of or all the issues in a case.

MOTION: A written or oral request asking the court for certain relief. For example, a party can request temporary child support or alimony pendente lite.

NONMARITAL PROPERTY: Separate property, property owned before marriage, or property acquired during the marriage by gift or inheritance.

ORDER: The court's ruling on any matters before it.

PETITION: A written document requesting certain relief from the court.

PLAINTIFF: The party who initiates a legal proceeding.

PLAN PARTICIPANT: The employed spouse who participates in a retirement benefits plan.

PLEADING: Any formal written document requesting relief from the court.

QDRO (QUALIFIED DOMESTIC RELATIONS ORDER): The written document provided for by federal law that directs or orders retirement benefits to be divided between spouses in divorce matters.

QMCSO (QUALIFIED MEDICAL CHILD SUPPORT ORDER): The written document provided for under federal law that requires group health insurance providers to give health coverage to children of an insured parent who is going through a divorce.

REHABILITATIVE ALIMONY: Money paid by one spouse to a lesser-paid or nonworking spouse for retraining or education. It is generally given for a finite period of time to enable the spouse to become financially independent.

RETAINER: An advance of legal fees.

RETAINER LETTER: A letter that should be written by a lawyer setting forth the terms of the legal representation.

SERVICE: The delivery of a legal document such as a divorce complaint or motion commencing a proceeding or requesting relief in the middle of a proceeding. Each state has specific rules that state how all documents must be served.

SETTLEMENT AGREEMENT: The written version of the agreement reached by the parties. Generally, it is best to reduce to writing the terms of any agreement reached between the parties as to how the property will be divided (or the terms of child custody, if applicable).

STIPULATION: An agreement between the parties or their counsel.

TRIAL: A formal court hearing in which all the outstanding disputed issues can be decided.

RESOURCES

LEGAL WEBSITES

There are many websites you may want to refer to when learning about divorce. It is always best to check the information you receive on a website with a lawyer before making any major decisions. One of the most comprehensive websites is Cornell Law School's, which can be found at www.law.cornell.edu.

The American Academy of Matrimonial Lawyers has a website that can help you get the name of a member of the Academy. There are also scholarly articles on divorce-related topics. Its website is www.aaml.org.

For legal resources, you might try www.findlaw.com. Another website you may find helpful is www.lawinfo.com.

Many law schools have websites with varying amounts of legal information. Many individual lawyers and law firms in each state maintain their own websites.

Nolo Press has a website that includes both self-help information and other legal information. It is www.nolo.com.

DIVORCE WEBSITES

Many websites contain financial information as well as tools that may help you calculate your financial support obligations. Again, keep in mind that the information you receive on these sites should be checked out with a professional in the area before you decide to act on the information you obtain.

The following are some websites on divorce:

www.divorcesource.com

www.divorcenet.com

www.divorceinfo.com

www.preciousheart.net (This site is a compendium of many divorce websites.)

www.divorcecentral.com

FINANCIAL RESOURCES

National Foundation for Credit Counseling (NFCC)
A national nonprofit network providing free or low-cost counseling and education on budgeting, credit, and debt resolution. To find a location near you, call 1-800-388-2227. Its website is www. nfc.org.

If you need a copy of past tax returns, you can call the Internal Revenue Service at 1-800-829-1040. Its website is www.irs.gov.

EXPERT ADVICE

To find a financial planner in your area:

Certified Financial Planner Board of Standards
1-888-237-6275
www.cfp-board.org

To help check if your financial planner is a Certified Financial Planner with a CFP designation:

Financial Planning Association
Atlanta, GA
1-800-647-6340
www.fpanet.org

To request a copy of a stockbroker's disciplinary and employment records:

National Association of Securities Dealers, Inc. (NASD)
1-800-289-9999
www.nasdr.com

ACTUARIES

To get information about actuaries:

American Academy of Actuaries
www.actuary.org

Society of Actuaries
www.soa.org

APPRAISERS

To get a list of accredited appraisers in your area:

American Society of Appraisers
Herndon, VA
1-800-272-8258
www.appraisers.org

National Association of Certified Valuation Analysts
1111 Brickyard Road, Suite 200
Salt Lake City, UT 84106-5401
1-801-486-0600
www.nacva.com

CREDIT

To check your credit rating, you may use any of the following:

Equifax
PO Box 74021
Atlanta, GA 30374-50241
1-800-685-1111
www.equifax.com

Experian
PO Box 2106
Allen, TX 75013-2104
1-888-Experian
www.experian.com

TransUnion
PO Box 403
Springfield, PA 19064-0390
1-800-888-4213
www.transunion.com

To find an enrolled agent in your area you can log on to the website www.naea.org.

INSURANCE

To obtain quotes for insurance rates:

Insurance Quote Services
1-800-972-1104
www.iquote.com

Life Insurance Services
1-888-622-0925
www.intelliquote.com

Quote Smith
1-800-431-1147
www.quotesmith.com

LOCATING LAWYERS

The following are organizations that may be helpful in finding a lawyer:

American Academy of Matrimonial Lawyers
150 North Michigan Avenue
Chicago, IL 60601
1-312-263-6477
www.aaml.org

American Bar Association
750 North Lake Shore Drive
Chicago, IL 60611
1-312-988-5000
www.abanet.org

Martindale Hubbell is a national directory of lawyers. Lawyers are
listed by geographical area and specialties.
www.lawyers.com

MEDIATORS

The following are a list of organizations you might contact for a
list of mediators:

Association for Conflict Resolution
1015 18th Street, N.W. 1150
Washington, D.C.
1-202-464-9700
www.acresolution.org

ACR is a merged organization of the American Academy of
Family Mediators, The Conflict Education Network, and the Society of Professional in Dispute Resolution.

The Association of Family and Conciliation Courts
1-608-664-3750
www.afccnet.org

Enclosed is a list of mediators nationwide:

California: Nina Meierding, 1-805-643-3543; Chip Rose,
1-408-429-9721

Illinois: Margaret S. Powers, 1-847-398-1969

Maryland: Carl D. Schneider, 1-301-565-8285; Stanley J. Rodbell, 1-410-730-2211; Louise Phipps Senft, 1-443-524-0833

Massachusetts: Diane Newman, 1-617-964-7485

New York: Adam J. Berner, 1-212-721-7555; Steven L. Abel, 1-914-634-4700

North Carolina: Jerry Bagnell, 1-910-784-1033

Oregon: Robert Benjamin, 1-503-417-2655

Pennsylvania: Susan V. Edwards, 1-610-725-0733; Edward Blumstein, 1-215-985-1001; Arnold Shienvold, 1-717-540-1313

Wisconsin: Allan R. Koritzinsky, 1-608-258-4275; Joan F. Kessler, 1-414-297-5541

Texas: Norma Levine Trusch, 1-713-961-0256; Donald Royall, 1-713-462-6500; Harry L. Tindall, 1-713-662-8733; Randall B. Wilhite, 1-713-986-7000

PENSIONS AND RETIREMENT

To find out about your or your spouse's Social Security benefits, contact the Social Security Administration.

1-800-772-1213
www.ssa.gov

There are many companies and individuals that prepare pension valuations. The following company is one example:

Pension Analysis Consultants, Inc.
1-800-288-3675
www.pensionanalysis.com

INDEX